T0288268

THE NEW SENTENCE

THE NEW SENTENCE

Ron Silliman

ROOF

FIFTH PRINTING.

ISBN: 978-0-937804-20-9
Library of Congress Catalog Card No.: 85-063543

Cover design by Lee Sherry.

These talks and essays first appeared, often in substantially different form, in the following periodicals: *American Book Review, Art Contemporary, The Difficulties, The Dumb Ox, L=A=N=G=U=A=G=E, Open Letter, Paideuma, Paper Air, Poetics Journal, Renegade, San Francisco Review of Books, Sulfur* and *Talks: Hills 6/7.* Some have appeared, at times abridged, in the following anthologies: *Claims for Poetry, In the American Tree, The L=A=N=G=U=A=G=E Book, The Poets' Encyclopedia* and *Writing/ Talks.* My thanks to the editors of these publications for their support o my work. "Towards Prose" is published here for the first time.

Roof Books are distributed by
Small Press Distribution
1341 Seventh Avenue
Berkeley, CA. 94710-1403.
Phone orders: 800-869-7553
www.spdbooks.org

 This book was made possible, in part, with public funds from the New York State Council on the Arts, a state agency.
NYSCA

ROOF BOOKS
are published by
Segue Foundation
300 Bowery
New York, NY 10012
www.roofbooks.com

CONTENTS

THE NEW SENTENCE

CONTEXTS

Because we think we can represent the world in language, we tend to imagine that the universe itself performs as one. Yet, if we look to that part of the world which is the poem, tracing the historical record of each critical attempt to articulate a poetics, a discursive account of what poetry might be, we find instead only metaphors, translations, tropes. That these models have a use should not be doubted—the relationships they bring to light, even when only casting shadows, can help guide our way through this terrain. Yet their value stands in direct relation to their provisionality, to the degree to which each paradigm is aware of itself as a translation of the real, inaccurate and incomplete.

My first critical writing came at a time when such activity was invariably associated with the academy or with that specific verse tradition which began with Pound and continued into the sixties through the work of Charles Olson and Robert Creeley. These later writers stood warily midway between the New Critics, whose positivist bias led toward an empiricist claim to transcendent (and trans-historical) truth, and other sectors of "New American" poetry whose anti-intellectualism was formed in part in opposition to the likes of Brooks and Warren. The disaster of America's war in Indochina made it painfully clear that poetry or any other serious pursuit which was not fundamentally critical bordered on suicidal behavior. What, in such circumstances, might then be the role for poetics?

Any response to this depends necessarily on one to yet another question: is the poet, by definition, an intellectual? I think the answer is yes. I am not claiming here that thought itself is reducible to language. The cognitive power of music or painting or dance can be every bit as great as the finest of poems. Nonetheless, language, and thus the poem, is inextricably involved with thought, and through this with the entire function of the intellectual, she for whom thinking is a ground for social practice. Writing itself is a form of action.

Necessarily, then, a poetics must be concerned with the process by which writing is organized politically into literature. It is particularly disturbing when, under the New Critics as well as Stalin, this transformation is posed and explained as though it were objective and not related directly to ongoing and fluid social struggles. Plural though they may be, today's canons are no less the product of an ultimately political impulse.

I offer these pieces then as both metaphors and interventions. I am aware that the tradition within which I work is an option that has been most readily available within the culture of educated, white men. That this does not represent the whole of society in no way invalidates its own legitimacy. If anything, it is imperative that we come to understand what this hegemonic tradition has meant, and may yet mean, within a larger sphere of action, even as we insist on the necessity of weaning it (or us) of its (or our) desire for domination.

This book consists of three sections and a coda. It was composed over eight years beginning in 1977. The first sequence addresses the poem's relation to society, the second the terrain of the poem itself, and the third the "mapping" which has been the site for my own practice as a poet. Six of the pieces began as talks, a form that reflects their creation within the San Francisco poetry scene of the late seventies and early eighties. Similar communities in New York, San Diego, Washington, D.C. and elsewhere have likewise played major roles. David Sternbach has worked over the course of a year to help shape this discourse into its current form. In some instances, his work was preceded by substantial editorial help from Bob Perelman and Barrett Watten.

Watten's impact in particular, as poet, critic and friend for the past 21 years, cannot be underestimated. I've found his demand for rigor and commitment to honesty unmatched in the world of poetry—indeed, in the world at large. This book's for him.

Vancouver
August, 1985

4

I ～～～～～～

DISAPPEARANCE OF THE WORD, APPEARANCE OF THE WORLD

> Human beings do not live in the objective world alone, nor alone in the world of social activity as ordinarily understood, but are very much at the mercy of the particular language which has become the medium of expression for their society. It is quite an illusion to imagine that one adjusts to reality essentially without the use of language and that language is merely an incidental means of solving specific problems of communication or reflection. The fact of the matter is that the 'real world' is to a large extent unconsciously built up on the language habits of the group.
> —Sapir, 1929

> The mode of production of material life conditions the social, political and intellectual life process in general. It is not the consciousness of men (*sic*) that determines their being, but on the contrary, their social being that determines their consciousness.
> —Marx, 1859

One anomaly of contemporary existence which has received little critical analysis is the persistence of "typos" in foreign language films from the industrialized nations. A typical example would be the omission of an *r* in the word "your" in Tanner's recent *Jonah who will be 25 in the Year 2000*. Since a film such as *Jonah* (or those directed by Truffaut, Bergman or Wertmuller) is made with at least one eye on distribution to the Anglo-American market, such errata cannot be sufficiently explained away as a consequence of the precarious and somewhat secondary existence of an export print (which, on occasion, is even re-edited for the new market, as was Roeg's *The Man Who Fell To Earth*). The fact remains that in current bourgeois cinema, attention to visual information is total. That the disruptive nature of typographical errors in sub-titles is not noticed and corrected is a sign that it is not felt.

This links it to a broad variety of other social phenomena, such as the method of speed-reading in which individual words recede and are replaced by a Gestalt comprehension of content, or the techniques developed for display advertising and product packaging (including mass market publishing) for the printing of information which, for any number of reasons (e.g., it is considered "inessential" such as the identification of the jacket designer, or possibly counterproductive to sales, such as a listing of chemical additives in canned foods), the producer does not wish the customer to read. In this sense the most revealing language in Noam Chomsky's *Reflections on Language* may well be the ISBN number on its rear cover, printed in a different direction and in a lighter color than the rest of that page's text.

These lingering traces of a would-be-invisible language mark a much greater transformation which has occurred over the past several centuries: the subjection of writing (and, through writing, language) to the social dynamics of capitalism. Words not only find themselves attached to commodities, they *become* commodities and, as such, take on the "mystical" and "mysterious character" Marx identified as the commodity fetish: torn from any tangible connection to their human makers, they appear instead as independent objects active in a universe of similar entities, a universe prior to, and outside, any agency by a perceiving Subject. A world whose inevitability invites acquiescence. Thus capitalism passes on its preferred reality through language itself to individual speakers. And, in so doing, necessarily effaces that original connecting point to the human, the perceptible presence of the signifier, the mark or sound, in the place of the signified.

8

To make this effacement clear, first we need to note some key differences in the language use of groups which have as yet not been completely incorporated into the class system of the modern world. Note, for example, that the presence of "nonsense" syllables in tribal literature is unmistakable. The following is an English language translation of a Fox tribe sweatbath poem:

A gi ya ni a gi yan ni i
A gi ya ni a gi yan ni i
A gi ya ni a gi yan ni i
A gi ya ni agi ya ni
Sky
A gi ya ni i a gi ya ni
A gi ya ni i a gi ya ni
A gi ya ni [1]

Save for attempts at specifically anthropological explanations, there is virtually no room in contemporary literary theory for a poetry of this kind, no existing mechanism for positing it coherently alongside the work of Dante, Li Po or Tzara. Even if one were to recognize in this surplus of sound the essence of Roman Jakobson's definition of the "poetic function," the focus on the signifier for its own sake, normative literary criticism stops far short, usually at the borders of the onomotopoetic, concluding instead, as do Wellek and Warren, that "mere sound in itself can have no or little aesthetic effect."[2] The fact that there have been as yet few attempts to incorporate such materials into "comparative literature" curricula by the educational systems of the industrial nations is not simply attributable to racism, though inevitably racism plays a role. Rather, it is that in the reality of capitalism, denying as it must any value in the purely gestural, that which serves solely to mark the connection between the product and its maker, the absence of any external reference is construed as an absence of meaning.

But capitalism did not spring up overnight amid loose associations of groups at a tribal stage of development. It came into existence through a long succession of stages, each with its own characteristic modes of production and social relations. Although much closer to our own modern experience than tribal poetry, the literature of people in these earlier stages of capitalism retains elements of this "meaningless" or gestural aspect of language. The following are the first eleven lines of "The Tunnying of Elynour Rummyng" by John Skelton, written in about 1517:

Tell you I chyll,
If that ye whyll
A whyle be styll,
Of a comely gyll
That dwelt on a hyll;
But she is not gryll,
For she is somewhat sage
And well worne in age,
For her vysage
It woldt aswage
A mannes courage.[3]

Only one word (*gryll* meaning "fierce") has dropped from the vocabulary. Shifts of spelling, pronunciation and syntactic structure are more visible (largely explicable by the standardizing effect of printing—Caxton's press was only forty years old when these lines were written), but the most obvious difference between Skelton's poetry, or that of any of his contemporaries, such as Sir Thomas More, and the modern is its use of rhyme: eleven consecutive end-rhymes using only two endings, *-yll* and *-age*, plus five other instances of internal rhyme and off-rhyme (*tell, whyle, dwelt, well, woldt*). This is the inverse of the effaced *r* of *Jonah*: it is an ordering of the language by its physical characteristics, its "non-linguistic" ones, a sign that this dimension *is felt*.

What happens when a language moves toward and passes into a capitalist stage of development is an anaesthetic transformation of the perceived tangibility of the word, with corresponding increases in its expository, descriptive and narrative capacities, preconditions for the invention of "realism," the illusion of reality in capitalist thought. These developments are tied directly to the function of reference in language, which under capitalism is transformed, narrowed into referentiality.

Reference possesses the character of the relationship of a movement to an object, such as the picking up of a stone to be used as a tool. Both movement and object carry their own integrities and are not confused: a sequence of gestures is distinct from the objects which may be involved, as distinct as the labor process is from its resultant commodities. A sequence of movements forms a discourse, not a depiction. It is precisely the expressive integrity of the gestural use of language which constitutes the meaning of the "nonsense" syllables in tribal poetries; its persistence in such characteristics of Skelton's poetry as its rhyme is that of a trace.

Within tribal societies the individual has not yet been reduced to wage labor, nor does material life require the consumption of a vast number of commodities, objects created through the work of others. Language likewise has not yet been transformed into a system of commodities, nor subjected to a division of labor in its functions through which the signified overwhelms the signifier. In contrast, where the bourgeois is the rising class, the expressive gestural, labor-product nature of consciousness tends to be repressed. Objects of consciousness, including individual words and even abstractions, are perceived as commodities and take on this "mystical" character of fetish. Missing here from the equation of reference is any recognition of the connection established by the signifier between the object or signified and the perceiving subject. Movement appears instead as though it were a feature of the object itself. Things which move freely, absent all gesture, are the elements of a world of depiction. Under the sway of the commodity fetish, language itself appears to become transparent, a mere vessel for the transfer of ostensibly autonymous referents. Thus, as Michael Reddy has documented, contemporary English is a language with no less than 141 metaphoric constructions in which communication itself is posed as a conduit. In Wittgenstein's classic formulation,

> A *picture* held us captive. And we could not get outside it, for it lay in our language and language seemed to repeat it to us inexorably.[4]

This social aphasia, the increasing transparency of language, took place in English over a period of not less than 400 years. Its most complete expression is perhaps in the genre of fictional realism, although it is hardly less pervasive in the presumed objectivity of daily journalism or the hypotactic logic of normative expository style. Thus in language as well as printing technology, the rise of capitalism set the preconditions for the rise of the novel.

For it is the disappearance of the word that lies at the heart of the invention of the illusion of realism and the breakdown of gestural poetic form.

Repression does not, fortunately, abolish the existence of the repressed element which continues as a contradiction, often invisible, in the social fact. As such, it continues to wage the class struggle of consciousness. The history of Anglo-American literature under capitalism is the history of this struggle. It can be discussed at many levels; I will outline only a few.

An event of significance is the development of books of poetry, usually dated in English by the publication of *Tottel's Miscellany* in 1557. If the very invention of the alphabet represents the initial, pre-capitalist, division of labor in language, the first movement of the language beyond the physical borders of the individual, and if the development of bards leads to a further division into a class of authors and a class of consumers, the arrival of the book greatly accelerates the process. From this moment forward, authors will see increasingly less of their audiences.

Another symptom of this gradual repression is the replacement, by 1750, of subjective styles of italicization and capitalization by "modern conventional" usage.

> The rather surprising thing is that so conspicuous and far-reaching a change should have evoked so little contemporary comment. The whole visual effect of a page of type is transformed by it. For us, this entails also a change in psychological response. Men do not ordinarily leave unremarked the swift departure of time-honored custom.[5]

But if the nature of this change is recognized as *repression*, a natural result of capitalist priorities in the social sphere, then such a conspiracy of silence is not surprising at all. By 1760 one writer, Edward Capell, had gone so far as to discontinue the capitalization of the initial letter of each line of the poem.

Even in the 18th century the contradictions of the commoditization of language resulted in counter-tendencies. The bourgeois English reader had to participate in the production of the book-as-object, for it was she who had to have it bound. Thus individual libraries were bound according to consumer aesthetic values, looking quite unlike the hodge-podge of colors and book sizes which typify the modern paperback home library. The sole trace of this counter-tendency in the modern era is the binding style used in encyclopedias and law books, intended to recall the style of that period.

Because of its singular adaptation to capitalist culture, the novel, a descendant of the poem whose generalization and acceptance as a form in Europe was a direct consequence of the invention of printing and extension of literacy beyond the borders of the clergy and ruling classes, is a primary source for any etiology of this fetishized reality. Of particular interest are the major forms of response to the modern "crisis" of the novel: the art-novel, the mass market novel and the movies. Before turning to these forms, some preliminary comments should be made concerning the nature of the serialized-language consumer and the inherently deformed relationship of the novel to its point of origin: the poem.

It was Sartre who argued that the two primary types of human relationships are the group and the series. The former is characteristic of tribal societies. Serialization (often termed alienation or atomization) places the individual as a passive cipher into a series of more or less identical units, Whitman's "simple separate person." Its apotheosis is to be found in the modern unemployment line. The function of the commoditized tongue of capitalism is the serialization of the language-user, especially the reader. In its ultimate form, the consumer of a mass market novel such as *Jaws* stares at a "blank" page (the page also of the speed-reader) while a story appears to unfold miraculously of its own free will before his or her eyes. The presence of language appears as recessive as the sub-title of a foreign language film.

The work of each poet, each poem, is a response to a determinate coordinate of language and history. Each writer possesses in his or her imagination a subjective conceptualization of this *matrix* (inevitably partial, inevitably a distortion), usually termed the tradition. The locus of the work to be written is felt as a blind spot, a primal lack toward which the writer is driven. This is the essential truth in the cliche that poets write only those poems which they *need*. Each successful poem abolishes (but only for a time) the lack and subtly reorganizes the structure of the subjective matrix.

Serialized language deforms this subjective perception. The hesitations and self-doubts about this, which fill *Tristram Shandy*, are increasingly anaesthetized by the rise of capitalism and appear not even to be felt by the modern pulp novelist who can just sit down and hack it out. (When felt, the consequence is often that phenomenon known as "writer's block.") For any Rex Stout, the movement of objects, absent the presence of any gestural element, presents no problem. Freed from recognition of the signifier and buffered against any response from an increasingly passive consumer, the supermarket novelist's language has become fully subservient to a process that would lie outside of syntax: plot. The dynamic implicit in the novel's rise toward the illusion of realism is this divorce, conducted in stages over centuries, of the tale from the gravitational force of language, an assumption that the free evolution of an art of the plot, as such, is possible. This dream of an art with no medium, of a signified with no signifiers, is inscribed entirely within the commodity fetish. Thus the seed of the modern "crisis of the novel"—the bankruptcy of normative realism announced by the advent of the modernists, and the subsequent marginalization of the mode as a social force in contemporary culture—was implanted at the very beginning, an inevitability inherent in the desire to cleave narrative from the gestural aspects of language. Instead of "freely" leaving the gravitational pull of the signifier, the novel, like a rocket with insufficient thrust, is doomed to fall back into the atmosphere of the poem: the peculiar affliction of Tyrone Slothrop is that of the novel itself.

Beginning with the early modernists, many novelists of serious intent at least sense the nature of this contradiction and attempt to confront it directly. Gertrude Stein attempts to reintroduce an anti-narrational continuous present. Hemingway strives for an art of the sentence as the novel's determining language-unit. Joyce attempts a frontal assault, the reintegration of the novel into language, but his is a pre-Saussurian linguistics, that of etymologies. Such approaches lead eventually to all manifestations of the contemporary art-novel. Of particular note within this vein is the appearance of a subdivision of novelists who write for, and are principally read by, poets, such as Jack Kerouac, Douglas Woolf, Paul Metcalf, Harry Matthews, Kathy Acker or Fielding Dawson.

Another tendency of response is to accept commoditization and to go on to write novels in which the language is all but invisible. While Saul Bellow (or Pearl Buck or John Steinbeck) represents an attempt to achieve this within a serious mode (the novel as a language art continuing to recall its prehistory in the poem, as art, while retaining virtually none of the poem's linguistic features), and while a number of other novelists merely stylize their acquiescence (Mailer, Vonnegut, Roth et al), more typical—and more revealing—are those who carry commoditization toward its logical conclusions in the mass-market best-seller, such as Leon Uris, Peter Benchley or Mario Puzo. Mickey Spillane, who simply *dictates* his novels, carries the disappearance-of-the-word/ appearance-of-the-world syndrome to its limit in writing.

In much the same manner as Stein, Joyce or Hemingway, every major western poetic movement has been an attempt to get beyond the repressing elements of capitalist reality, toward a whole language art. Typically, they have been deformed at the outset by the very condition of existing within the confines of the dominant reality. The dream narratives of surrealism, because they were narratives, could never hope to go beyond the fetish of plot, as hopelessly trapped within it as "socialist realism." The entire projective tendency, from Pound to Robert Kelly, attempts to rediscover a physical ordering of the language, but posits that order not within the language but within individuals (individualism is the codification of serialized "man"), operating on the metaphoric equation of a page as scored speech. Contemporary poets such as Clark Coolidge or Robert Grenier frontally attack referentiality, but only through negation by specific context. To the extent that negation is determined by the thing negated, they too operate within the larger fetish.

Likewise, a history of literary *criticism* could be written, identifying its origins also within the poem, its exteriorizing serialization and the resolution of its subsequent crisis through state subsidy by its implantation into the university structure, a process of bureaucratization through which writing is transformed into the canon of Literature. Such a history would begin with a definition of the function of literary criticism as the separation of the self-consciousness of the activity of the poem from the poem itself. It would locate the necessity for this separation in the repressive element of the serialization of language as it functions within a capitalist epoch. It would explore in depth the role of a bureaucratized criticism in a capitalist society as the creation of a "safe" and "official" culture through its self-restriction of the object of inquiry to a small number of works identified as the national literature. It would study the illusion of clarity in criticism in its use of the essay form, in which the contradictions of its existence, such as would be revealed through inarticulations, redundancies and non-sequiturs, are subsumed under hypotactic form, rendered invisible rather than resolved. Finally it would study the existence of counter-tendencies within literary criticism as well, specifically the sometimes anarchic works of literary theory created by poets (e.g., the body of prose left by Charles Olson) and the recent trend in France toward literary criticism as an admitted art form (e.g., Roland Barthes or Jacques Derrida).

This process, the overwhelming of the signifier by the signified, the increasing transparency of form in the face of an ever more hierarchically organized content, is not limited to what are normally recognized as the language arts. Taking advantage of a technological development, capitalism's classic defense mechanism, the impulse toward a plot-centered art imposed itself on a new and still unformed medium, creating out of film something called the "motion picture." The movies lent theater all of the advantages of the novel: a greater range in scenery, the potential for rapid changes in time or place, a medium whose signifiers were more easily hidden than the backdrop of a stage (one thinks more in terms of characters than of light, space, time or sound), and, not incidentally, the serialization of the consumer through the reproducibility of prints. What the movies took from theatre was not merely its labor pool, but also its highly specialized mode of social organization. Ironically perhaps, the highly stratified form of the modern film company finds itself reflected in the contemporary corporate publishing house, where "teams" of authors (contract employees producing on a piece-work basis) churn out "novelizations" of popular movies. In cinema as elsewhere, counter-tendencies exist, reflecting the fact that this type of social organization, and that this particular presentation of reality, is not inherent in the medium itself. Just as the *auteur* theory of film criticism attempted to create a recognition of the relation between a product and its maker, structuralist or "avant garde" personal cinema, often produced without a significant division of labor, provides its consumers with a plentitude of signifiers. Like the "social realists" of the novel a generation ago, documentaries of the independent left essentially accept the fetishism of a plot-centered art (although they are more apt to make note of this fact in a Brechtian fashion). They focus their oppositional energies on the messages instead conveyed to a consumer, whose passivity they challenge without recognizing that it is an acquiescence constituted by the very process itself.

Yet it is in the poem that the implications of this process, and of any possible solutions, most clearly need to be delineated. The poem is not only the point of origin for all the language and narrative arts, the poem returns us to the very social function of art as such: for the group, art interiorizes its consciousness by the ordering (one could call it "tuning") of individual sense perceptions; for the individual, be it artist or consumer, art provides her with experiences of that dialectical consciousness in which subject and object, self and other, individual and group, unite. Since it is precisely this dialectical consciousness which capitalism seeks to repress through the serialization of the individual (for it is by such consciousness that we know the overdetermination of the objects of our existence by the capitalist mode of production), the fine arts in general function as deformed counter-tendencies within the dominant society. Perhaps only due to its historical standing as the first of the language arts, poetry has yielded less to (and resisted more) this process of capitalist transformation. It remains, for example, the only genre in which spelling may be unconventional without a specific narrative justification.

It is the task of dialectical analysis to not merely explain the social origin and underlying structure of phenomena, but to ground them in the present social fact of class and other struggles so as to indicate appropriate courses of action. The social role of the poem places it in an important position to carry the class struggle *for* consciousness to the level *of* consciousness. It is clear that one cannot change language (or consciousness) by fiat: the French Academy has only succeeded in limiting vocabulary. First there must be a change in the mode and control of production of material life.

By recognizing itself as the *philosophy of practice in language*, poetry can work to search out the preconditions of a liberated language within the existing social fact. This requires (1) recognition of the historic nature and structure of referentiality, (2) placing the issue of language, the repressed signifier, at the center of the program, and (3) placing the program into the context of conscious class struggle. Such poetry will take as its motto the words of Marx's *The Eighteenth Brumaire of Louis Bonaparte:*

> The social revolution . . . cannot draw its poetry from the past, but only from the future.

RE WRITING: MARX

The poetry of societies in which the capitalist mode of production prevails appears as an "immense collection of books"; the individual book appears as its elementary form. Our investigation begins with the analysis of the book.

The book is, first of all, an external object, a thing which through its qualities satisfies human needs of a literary kind.

Objects of reading become books only because they are the products of the writing of private individuals who work independently of each other. The sum total of the writing of all these private individuals forms the aggregate writing of society. *Since the writers do not come into social contact until they exchange the products of their writing*, the specific social characteristics of their private writings appear only within this exchange. In other words, the writing of the private individual manifests itself as an element of the total writing of society *only through the relations* which the act of exchange establishes between the texts, and, through their mediation, between the writers. To the writers, therefore, the social relations between their private writing appear as what they are, *i.e.*, they do not appear as direct social relations between persons in their work, but rather as material relations between persons and social relations between texts.

However, a text can be useful, and a product of human writing, without being a book. She who satisfies her own need with the text of her own writing admittedly creates reading-values, but not books. In order to produce the latter, she must not only produce reading-values, *but reading-values for others*, social reading-values. And not merely for others. In order to become a book, the text must be transferred to the other person, for whom it serves as a reading-value, *through the medium of exchange.*

THE POLITICAL ECONOMY OF POETRY

for San Francisco DSA

Poems both are and are not commodities. It is the very partialness of this determination which makes possible much of the confusion among poets, particularly on the left, as to the nature of their participation in (including, perhaps, opposition to) commodity capitalism through the process of making art. Any commodity is necessarily an object and has a physical existence, even if this aspect is no more than the vibrating vocal chords of a sound poet. But not all objects are commodities. That which exists in nature and has a use, such as water, is a good—the hiker comes to the stream and drinks. Only that which is *produced* for its utility achieves the status of product (the water is piped to a metropolitan reservoir and filtered). Of products, only those which are *made for exchange* (and specifically exchange for money) become commodities (Perrier).

The writer who composes a work and reveals it to no one, keeping it instead confined to her notebook, nonetheless has created a product which possesses real use value (part of which may be in the writing process) for its lone consumer. Likewise, two poets trading photocopies of their latest works are exchanging products. And even to the extent that a small press edition of a book of poems may have a certain portion of its run set aside for the author in lieu of royalties, and that many of those copies will be given away, it also will suffer a divided identity.

Yet books and texts do not exist at quite the same level, nor are they produced by exactly the same people. Further muddying the situation is the subsidization, however minimal, in most of the

English-speaking nations of both writers and publications by the state. To what degree can we use the term commodity to describe a book sold in a store when its publisher has no hope of recouping her original costs, and when these losses will be at least partly absorbed by a third party? Is its commodification nothing more than a strategy for maximum circulation, so that the volume might achieve a greater product-function? Should government patronage be seen as a metaconsumption, in which what is purchased is not textual, but simply the existence of poets and poetry as an ornament to the national culture?

Perhaps, but more important to the equation is the simple presence of consumption, for the role it plays, however dimly perceived by individual authors, in motivating the productions of texts *for exchange*. It was just this which Laura Riding discovered in her 1926 essay "T.E. Hulme, the New Barbarism, & Gertrude Stein,"[1] when she complained of "the forced professionalization of poetry." The poet who writes with the idea of having her poems published, of having them collected into books and distributed through stores and direct mail purchases (which may at this point be the larger sector of the market), has inescapably been drawn into the creation of commodities.

The book, *a commodity*, radically alters the composition and potential size of an audience. Yet, although literary theory since the time of the New Critics has done much to elaborate the possible meanings in a given text, it has remained essentially silent about the relations of the social features of any actual, particular audience in the creation of such meanings. This absence banishes any serious consideration of the ideological component, which is reduced instead to a question of the politics of the writer or those of individual characters (an example would be Terry Eagleton's discussion of George Eliot in *Criticism and Ideology*[2]).

The role of the reader in the determination of a poem's ideological content is neither abstract nor beyond the scope of feasible examination. The question is contextual, not textual. As early as 1929, Valentin Vološinov *wrote:*

The actual reality of language-speech is not the abstract system of linguistic forms, not the isolated monologic utterance, and not the psychophysiological act of its implementation, but the social event of verbal interaction implemented in an utterance or utterances.

Thus, verbal interaction is the basic reality of language . . . . A book, i.e., *a verbal performance in print* is also an element of verbal communication. It is something discussable in actual, real-life dialogue, but aside from that, it is calculated for active perception, involving attentive reading and inner responsiveness, and for organized, *printed* reaction . . . (book reviews, critical surveys, defining influence on subsequent works, and so on). Moreover, a verbal performance of this kind also inevitably orients itself with respect to previous performances in the same sphere, both those by the same author and those by other authors. It inevitably takes its point of departure from some particular state of affairs . . . . Thus the printed verbal performance engages, as it were, in ideological colloquy of large scale: it responds to something, objects to something, affirms something, anticipates possible responses and objections, seeks support, and so on.

Any utterance, no matter how weighty and complete in and of itself, *is only a moment in the continuous process of verbal communication.* But that continuous verbal communication is, in turn, itself only a moment in the continuous, all-inclusive, generative process of a given social collective . . . . *Verbal communication can never be understood and explained outside of this connection with a concrete situation.*[3]

Contrast Vološinov's perspective with that of New Critics René Wellek and Austin Warren: "the real poem must be conceived as a structure of norms, realized only partially in the experience of its many readers." Their argument in *Theory of Literature*, 1942, is a thorough assault on all contextual approaches:

What is the 'real' poem; where should we look for it; how does it exist . . . ?

One of the most common and oldest answers is the view that a poem is an 'artefact', an object of the same nature as a piece of sculpture or a painting. Thus the work of art is considered identical with the black lines of ink on white paper or parchment or, if we think of a Babylonian poem, with the grooves in the brick. Obviously this answer is quite unsatisfactory. There is, first of all, the huge oral 'literature'. There are poems or stories which have never been fixed in writing and still continue to exist. Thus the lines in black ink are merely a method of recording a poem which must be conceived as existing elsewhere. If we destroy the writing or even all copies of a printed book we still may not destroy the poem . . . . Besides, not every printing is considered by us, the readers, a correct printing of a poem. The very fact that we are able to correct printer's errors in a text which we might not have read before or, in some rare cases, restore the genuine meaning of the text shows that we do not consider the printed lines as the genuine poem. Thus we have shown that the poem (or any literary work of art) can exist outside its printed version and that the printed artefact contains many elements which we all must consider as not included in the genuine poem.[4]

While the Saussurean bias against writing as anything more than a shadow of speech is evident enough in this classic passage, more telling (at least for its impact on subsequent literary theory) is the demand of a single aspect of the work which can be elevated to the status of *genuine*. In the cause of textual analysis, Wellek and Warren succeeded in delegitimating the fuller study of literature as a total social process.

This is not to be confused with the dialectical method of moving from the concrete to the abstract, from the printed poem to its social context, in order to identify principles and structures with which to return to concrete practice. Wellek and Warren's idealization of the text is a complete rupture, achieved by a stylistic sleight of hand (writing is only a record of speech, yet oral work is only literature in quotes, severing the text from any material finality). This dematerialization conspires to make "possible the continuity of literary tradition" and "increase the unity . . . of works of art" by banishing investigations of difference at other levels.

The career of William Carlos Williams demonstrates the real consequences of those aspects of literary production and consumption which New Criticism would dismiss. Many young poets today feel that his finest work is to be found in *Spring & All* and the other books composed between 1920 and '32. Yet several of the 'New American' poets of the 50s are on record as having been primarily influenced by Williams' 1944 collection *The Wedge*. This means that young writers perceive the stamp of Williams' example, teaching and prestige on the work of their immediate predecessors as having a value other than that presumed by those somewhat older poets. A poet who bears that mark heavily, such as Lew Welch, is apt to become marginalized by the process.

Spring & All was not available in the 1950s, though the poems in it were included (in an altered order) in *The Collected Earlier Poems*. To be certain, the texts themselves did not change, but their inaccessibility blocked communication, and by the time Harvey Brown's Frontier Press brought them back to a possible public, the audience itself had been transformed: in addition to their having experienced a greatly expanded educational system in the 60s, a war in Viet Nam which had already gone sour, and the familiarity with psychedelics, the new readers of *Spring & All* had often already assimilated the work of Olson, O'Hara, Creeley and others.

An even clearer example of the literary (and therefore social) difference of different editions can be found in Jim Carroll's *Basketball Diaries*, a teenage memoir of sex, drugs and rock-n-roll which over 15 years went through piecemeal appearances in little poetry magazines, a slick small press edition, and finally emerged as a mass market paperback—reviewed and even excerpted in the nation's *sports* pages. At one end of this spectrum is a group of readers who found in Carroll a natural, even primitive, tough-lyric prose style, embodying many of the principles held by writers associated with the Saint Mark's Church in New York and articulated most forcefully by Ted Berrigan. At the other end is a group of readers who probably have never heard of Ted Berrigan and for whom the considerations of style, without which the *Diaries* would never have been printed, are utterly beside the point.

Even in cases, such as live performance, where the author is present, different audiences will receive and interpret a given work differently. In a talk given at San Francisco's 80 Langton Street, Robert Glück offers this example:

> At several Movement readings I was interested to see members of the audience come up afterwards and say where the writer had got it right (yes, that's my life) and where the writer had got it wrong. I want to contrast this with the audience that admires writing as if it were a piece of Georgian silver, goods to be consumed. Of course this depends on an identification with a community, a shared ideology. For example, I read a story at a gay reading about being 'queer-bashed.' The audience responded throughout with shouts of encouragement and acknowledgement. Afterwards people told me I got it right. I read the same story to an appreciative and polite university audience, and afterwards people told me they admired my transitions. To a certain extent, my story registered only in terms of form.[5]

Although Glück foregrounds here the role of context, he implicitly reproduces the Wellek-Warren presumption of 'correctness,' merely substituting a preferred definition (one which avoids addressing the *political* question of what is accomplished by correctness: the delegitimization of something, and by fiat, not argument). His characterization of an "audience that admires writing as if it were a piece of Georgian silver" is in fact incorrect, because he omits the fact that the second group's response is conditioned by their identification with Glück *as a writer* (and/or as an intellectual *because* he writes). What is shared is not the experience of homophobic violence, but the problems of a craft.

What can be communicated through any literary production depends on which codes are shared with its audience. The potential contents of the of the text are only actualized according to their reception, which depends on the social composition of the receivers. The work of Clark Coolidge, for example, might seem opaque and forbidding at a gay reading, for the same reason that a Japanese speaker cannot communicate with an Italian: no codes are shared from which to translate from word to meaning. There may be several people at a gay reading who are as interested as Coolidge in geology, bebop, Salvador Dali, weather, and even the same kinds of writing problems, but these concerns are not what bring people to such an event.

The social composition of its audience is the primary context of any writing. Context determines (and is determined by) both the motives of the readers and their experience, their history, i.e., their particular set of possible codes. Context determines the actual, real-life consumption of the literary product, without which communication of a message (formal, substantive, ideological) cannot occur. It tells us very little to know only that one group was a "gay reading" and the other a "university audience." A school with a large English department and a creative writing major is entirely different from a school focusing on science and agriculture. A reading to a graduate level class in rhetoric is not the same as another to the general student body.

It is here, at the question of context, a place that does not even exist within the system of Wellek and Warren, that both Riding and Glück complain in their very different ways of the "forced professionalization" of poetry. We can see here also that the

"continuity of literary tradition" and the "unity . . . of works of art"
is not a partial truth, but a calculated fabrication that expresses
more clearly than its authors could have known, the ideology of late
capitalism. Their "us, the readers," able to determine "a correct
printing of a poem" and capable of restoring "the genuine meaning
of the text" is not just any reader, but a particular one, unnamed,
with a particular education and occupation. Glück's argument
(although it fails to distinguish between the worker's concern for
the quality and manufacture of her product and the attitude of a
collector of Georgian silver) is an improvement to the degree that
his naming of a "best reader" at least acknowledges the existence of
other audiences.

The New Critics, however, were not solely responsible for the
illusion of a "continuity of literary tradition" made possible by the
banishment of other readers. Their task was to give this mirage a
cloak of critical respectability. Wellek and Warren's comments, it
should be noted, came during the long four-and-one-half decade
period (1911–1955) when the number of book titles published in
the United States per year remained relatively static at under
12,000,[6] in spite of the emergence of large corporate publishing
firms, while membership in the Modern Language Association
(MLA) rose from 1,047 to 8,453.[7] In short, the rise of a professional
caste of "specialized" or, more accurately, bureaucratized readers
occurred precisely at the moment when a new set of dynamics,
characterized by such concepts as market position, penetration and
share, began to reorganize the distribution of what had for a long
time been a fixed output. Thus corporate collaboration with the
leadership of this new caste at least appeared to offer commanding
control over the future of the market itself.

It was, more than anything else, the affluence of the U.S. after
the Second World War which kept this "promise" from being met.
New offset printing technology lowered the cost of book
production, permitting the large publishers to further segment
their markets and realize profits from an increased diversity of
titles, while simultaneously enabling a dramatic expansion in the
number of small, independent producers. Similarly, post-Sputnik
higher education brought new masses into what had previously
been the terrain of a more homogenous, class-determined few.
Membership in the MLA (itself much more diversified) was to peak
in 1971 at 31,356, while the number of book titles published per

year now exceeds 40,000. Finally, beginning with the creation of the Literature Panel of the National Endowment for the Arts in 1966, state subsidies for poets and the publication of poetry became an active force in the decentralization of literature. The rise of the "New American" poetries and their successors, as well as that of writing coming out of the women's movement, and from ethnic and sexual minority communities, can be viewed as a consequence of these social and technological transformations, each of which, in turn, is grounded in economic circumstance.

Yet, even with subsidies, there is not enough capital in the entire poetry industry to directly support poets and publishers. This partly determines who will be poets, and at what period of their lives poets are more apt to be active and publish. More importantly, however, this means that nearly all poets will turn elsewhere to make a living. Thus poets as a group have a wide range of jobs. This in turn means both that poets see work (and the politics of the workplace) in a non-uniform manner from a variety of perspectives and are less likely to perceive poetry as work (at least in the sense of the politics which would extend from that perception). It also partly explains why so much of the discussion of the politics of literature has been fixated on the lone aspect of content.

"Professional" poets include individuals who come from the entire spectrum of economic classes. The actual number of those who might accurately be described as bourgeois is small, and it is speculative to suggest that it exceeds the 2% figure which holds for the general U.S. population. The neobeatnik/neodada/street poet scene which manifests itself in every major urban center, on the other hand, might be characterized by the lumpen orientation of many of its participants. But the vast majority of poets fall in between. While many are traditionally working class and while there may be a somewhat higher concentration of classically-defined petty bourgeois than in the general American economy, a significant concentration of poets falls into a category that the late Nicos Poulantzas called The New Petty Bourgeoisie:

> This is also where the current devaluation of educational certificates and attainments is most important, given the significance that these have on the labour market and for the promotion chances of these agents. It can be seen in the currently massive occupation of subaltern posts by agents whose educational qualifications led them

to have different aspirations. In actual fact, this is the fraction into which young people holding devalued university degrees gravitate on a massive scale. It leads to the various forms of disguised unemployment that ravages this fraction: various forms of illegal work, vacation work, temporary and auxiliary work. These affect all those fractions with an objectively proletarian polarization, but are particularly pronounced in this case.[8]

Poets, for obvious reasons, tend to look at "disguised unemployment" as time to write, which partly explains their gravitation to part-time service sector jobs, such as clerking in bookstores or proofreading for publishers and law firms. Poulantzas also notes that

> It now seems, however, as if the last few years have seen the development, in the majority of capitalist countries, of an actual mental labour reserve army, over and above any cyclical phenomena.[9]

Poulantzas, however, has a very restricted class model, considering mental work and service sector employment to be unproductive, and therefore excluded from the working class as such (although conceding the "objectively proletarian polarization"). Still, the description, especially with regard to the under-utilized education and partial employment, is a close fit to the lives of many American poets under 40.

Erik Olin Wright, one of Poulantzas' most vigorous critics, uses a more complex model in which this same group is categorized as working class yet with a strong degree of contradiction as to class allegiance. Noting that more than 30% of economically active Americans had, by 1969, come into the "unproductive mental" labor sector, Wright notes that

> The contradictory locations around the boundary of the working class represent positions which do have a real interest in socialism, yet simultaneously gain certain real privileges directly from capitalist relations of production.[10]

Situated within these complex and sometimes contradictory economic relations, the social organization of contemporary poetry occurs in two primary structures: the *network* and the *scene*. The scene is specific to a place. A network, by definition, is transgeographic. Neither mode ever exists in a pure form. Networks typically involve scene subgroupings, while many scenes (although not all) build toward network formations. Individuals may, and often do, belong to more than one of these informal organizations at a time. Both types are essentially fluid and fragile. As the Black Mountain poets and others have demonstrated, it is possible for literary tendencies to move through both models at different stages in their development.

Critical to the distinction between these structures are the methods of communication available to their members. A sociology of poetry, noting, for example, that a reading series requires far less start-up capital than either a book or magazine, or that the face-to-face interactions which take place in such settings seldom demand the initiative needed to begin a serious, long-distance correspondence with a stranger, would correlate such implications with the class backgrounds and orientations of both writers and readers, real and potential alike. Yet, if such a sociology is not to fall prey to technological determinism, it must ask not simply which methods of interaction are in use, but, more importantly, to what end. Because capital, of which there is so little in poetry, is necessary for the elements of network formation, competition exists between networks and scenes. Underneath lies a hidden assumption of the hierarchical ordering of these groups, and the idea that one can be the dominant or hegemonic formation according to some definition, at least for a period of time. Definitions vary, but major components include monetary rewards, prestige (often called influence), and the capacity to have one's work permanently in print and being taught.

Here the role of trade publishing and its allies is completely clear. Trade presses may produce less than 4% of all poetry titles, but in an anthology such as *The American Poetry Anthology*[11] they represent 54% of all books used as sources for the collection. University presses contributed another 31%. Nearly half of the remaining small press books came from Ecco Press, the editor's own imprint.

Trade publishing is the metanetwork of American poetry. It is the contemporary manifestation of the academic network that Wellek and Warren argued for more than 30 years ago, and university employment remains a primary social feature. But, because this is the network which is aligned with capital, it can and does incorporate poets from other groups on a token basis. While this serves to give them much broader distribution, they in turn legitimate the metanetwork, masking to some degree its very network structure.

This alliance with capital yields another major advantage: the relative efficiency of trade distribution virtually guarantees its predominance on college course reading lists, *which is the largest single market for books of poetry*, with 2500 colleges and 200 writing programs in North America.

So long as capital, in the form of corporate publishers, can substantially determine the distribution of poetry in its major market, and so long as Daniel Halpern can call a collection of their network *The American Poetry Anthology* without challenge, this type of hegemony is not apt to be broken. The competition between other networks and scenes amounts to little more than jockeying for the token slots in the metanetwork.

But this is neither the only mode of hegemony, nor necessarily the most important. Here the question is not whether a poet will be read in five or fifty or five hundred years, but whether that poet can and will be read by individuals *able and willing to act* on their increased understanding of the world as a result of the communication. A poetics whose ultimate motive is nothing more than the maintenance of its own social position within a status quo reaches such an audience only insofar as it fosters no action whatsoever. The inclusion of blacks and feminists in the Halpern anthology functions precisely to keep the readers of those poets from questioning the presence of the white male college teachers who dominate the book.

What a consciously oppositional writer such as Robert Glück fails to consider when he dismisses one of his audiences in favor of the other is that their social composition is not identical. Any definition of response needs to be tailored accordingly. In part, this problem may reflect Glück's own overlapping membership in each community. It is, however, a major characteristic of the social codes of just those formations most often apt to attend a college reading not to know or speak their own name. In labelling that audience consumers, Glück forgets that consumption *for further production* is a moment of production itself—it *is* action. It is through the question of transitions, for example, that the "seamlessness" (i.e., the "natural" or "inevitable" quality) of perceived reality, including

30

that of the "continuity of literary tradition," might be revealed as the affect of a partisan ideological construct. A construct, in fact, which might also yield, as parallel states of "the inevitable," the social omnipotence of capital and the relative superiority of bourgeois (as distinct from economic) democracy as a method for governance in an imperfect world.

Still, just identifying Glück's university audience as a coalition of writers, teachers and specialized readers falls short of connecting them to the larger social orders of which they are a strategic fragment. This self-invisibility has parallels throughout contemporary life. It has only been through the struggle of non-whites, of women and of gays that the white male heterosexual has come into recognition of his own, pervasive presence. In poetry, there continues to be a radical break between those networks and scenes which are organized by and around the codes of oppressed peoples, and those other "purely aesthetic" schools. In fact, the aesthetics of those latter schools is a direct result of ideological struggle, both between networks and scenes, and within them. It is characteristic of the class situation of those schools that this struggle is carried on *in other (aesthetic) terms*.

Poetry in America reflects struggle carried out, unfortunately, in an unorganized and often individualist manner. This struggle is as much one between audiences as it is between poets (or, to be precise, it is one between social formations, including, but never limited to, economic classes, from which audiences are composed around individual authors). It is class war—and more—conducted through the normal social mechanisms of verse. The primary ideological message of poetry lies not in its explicit content, political though that may be, but in the *attitude toward reception* it demands of the reader. It is this "attitude toward information," which is carried forward by the recipient. It is this attitude which forms the basis for a response to other information, not necessarily literary, in the text. And, beyond the poem, in the world.

BENJAMIN'S AURA

> You should be alone when you listen to
> music, on the radio or on records, or
> played by three or four friends. To listen
> surrounded by a crowd of people who are
> also listening is pointless. Music is made
> to be listened to by each person
> individually.
>
> —Sartre[1]

When Walter Benjamin undertook his critique of the
reproducibility of art through technology, this mode was in its
infancy: the 20th century transformation of technology had barely
begun. The shift from the Taylorized routine of the automotive
assembly-line to the "instantaneous" international transfer of disk-
stored data via modems, microwave transmitters and satellite
relays, which could hardly have been foreseen in 1936, is only one of
several "external" factors which inject themselves subtly into any
contemporary reading of Benjamin's brief, decisive essay, "The
Work of Art in the Age of Mechanical Reproduction."[2] This article,
more of a sketch or pastiche than a completed analysis (a condition
characteristic of much of his writing), took 32 years to reach its
audience in English translation, arriving at a moment when the
rather different manifestoes of Marshall McLuhan set the stage for
Benjamin's immediate, if posthumous, canonization. If, in his own
brief lifetime, Benjamin had merely been a peripheral figure within
the Frankfurt School and a thorn in the side of Lukács, his writing
now found itself at the center of a new generation of critical

thinking, most notably in the books of John Berger, Susan Sontag and Terry Eagleton, whose extensions of their master's practice must further mediate any attempt to recapture the intentions of the original work. Then, too, the Marxism which had begun to re-emerge in the arts and academy in the late 1960s after a generation of forced absence under McCarthyism, was a far cry from that which greeted Benjamin, Adorno, Horkheimer, Marcuse and their friends in the thirties. The very same oppositionality to Stalinist state capitalism which had once marginalized the Frankfurt School within the European Marxist movement now enabled a new generation of progressives, as thoroughly distrustful of the Soviet Union's imperialism as of the United States', to find through Critical Theory a new Marx, that of the *Grundrisse*, humanist, dialectical, no friend of the bureaucratic state.

Nor is Marxism the only critical discourse to have changed dramatically in the 48 years since "The Work of Art" first appeared. Just as Jacques Lacan has demonstrated how differently Freud's work might have emerged had the vocabulary of linguistics been available to him, so Benjamin might have found much postwar French literary theory, particularly Barthes' elaboration of semiology and Derrida's critique of presence and absence, useful in unpacking such fundamental notions as *aura* and *authenticity*. Benjamin not only shares a range of concerns with structuralism ("The Work of Art" is to photography and film what *Writing Degree Zero* is to literature), but also a sense of the importance of material and social context (which Benjamin usually calls 'tradition'), an attitude inherited from the Russian Formalists. Criticism is only now beginning to comprehend that context is the antidote to the metaphysics of identity. Had Benjamin been able to raise certain issues, such as the privilege of visual representation, within "The Work of Art," Derrida's diacritical (anti-dialectical) formulations in these areas might never have seemed necessary. Written 30 years later, however, they release the seeds of Benjamin's thought.

The first words of "The Work of Art" belong to Paul Valéry. Their tone, quite unlike what is to follow, combines astonishment with tacit approval:

> the amazing growth of our techniques, the adaptability and precision they have attained, the ideas and habits they are creating, make it a certainty that profound changes are impending in the ancient craft

of the Beautiful. *In all the arts there is a physical component which can no longer be considered or treated as it used to be,* which cannot remain unaffected by our modern knowledge and power. . . . We must expect great innovations to transform the entire technique of the arts . . . .[3]

That there existed a physical component in the production of each art was itself an insight into the transformations which the various media were undergoing. Neither Whitman, say, in his preface to the first edition of *Leaves of Grass* (1855), nor Wordsworth in his preface to the second edition of *Lyrical Ballads* (1800), even approach such a consideration. For both, poetry was a mode of speech written down. Whitman uses the terms 'bard' and 'priest' as synonyms for 'poet.' Wordsworth writes:

what is meant by the word Poet? What is a Poet? To whom does he (*sic*) address himself? And what language is to be expected from him? — He is a man speaking to men . . . .[4]

Valéry was a youth when Mallarmé utilized different typefaces to indicate volume, pitch, super- and subtexts in the 1897 poem, *Un Coup de Dés* (A Throw of the Dice), acknowledging for the first time something which had increasingly been the case since Gutenberg's Vulgate of 1456, that the page in poetry had become a page of type. When, soon thereafter, Ezra Pound sat down at the typewriter, he gave rise to modern verse in English. Gradually, the page became an active presence *within* the poem itself, in a way which had only been hinted at previously in Mallarmé, the shaped poems of Herbert or Blake's illuminated manuscripts. This gradual recognition of the physical was not restricted to literature. Cubist painters started to supplement their canvases with elements taken from the "real" world in 1911, a gesture with much farther reaching consequences than their analytic reduction of visual perception.

The use of a quotation as an opening flourish is a mark of the literary. It instantly associates "The Work of Art" with a genre and tradition, thereby creating a specific set of expectations. This cautionary measure is justified on two counts. First, the frames of the essay, its preface and epilogue, place the piece into what was, in 1936, a minority faction of aesthetic criticism, Marxism. By pointing to a lack within the Marxist canon, Benjamin risked having his thesis rejected by non-Marxists as Marxian, and by

Marxists as pseudo- or anti-Marxian. Second, the structure of what is contained between those frames is decidedly unusual, resembling a discourse, perhaps a speech cued by notecards, more than the orderly, closed outline of normative expository practice. The essay does not lead so much as it flows in short sections of concentrated ideas.

The preface, aiming to justify Benjamin's argument within a Marxist frame, rests upon three assertions. The first is that "When Marx undertook his critique of the capitalistic mode of production, this mode was in its infancy."[5] While such a statement ignores evidence that capitalism had been emerging, even manifest, for several hundred years, it does distinguish between early, or free market, capitalism and the later industrial version. This evolution of capitalism entails more than an increase in the quantity of misery: Benjamin writes, "one could expect it not only to exploit the proletariat with increasing intensity, but ultimately to create conditions which would make it possible to abolish capitalism itself."[6] The fineness of this distinction, between oppression and revolutionary possibility, takes on depth in the second of Benjamin's founding assertions:

> The transformation of the superstructure, which takes place far more slowly than that of the substructure, has taken more than half a century to manifest in all areas of culture the changes in the conditions of production.[7]

Reading the text of daily life according to Marxist principles is doubly difficult: the object in front of us is not the same as that which confronted Marx, nor can we be certain the evidence of practical experience accurately represents underlying relationships as they currently exist. We are faced with tackling what we cannot see with tools fashioned under other conditions, regardless of the parallels in purpose. Benjamin's optimism is understandably restrained: the abolishment of capitalism is not inevitable, only "possible."

Benjamin's presumption of this occultation of the meaning of perceived experience has significant consequences in that, for him, any statement of direct observation must be *a priori* suspect. Failure or refusal to recognize this can lead the reader of "The Work of Art", sympathetic or not, to view its argument as the result of a mystical or subterranean process. Thus John Berger writes:

> The structuring of his thought was theological and Talmu-
> dic. . . .[8]

While Fredric Jameson proposes that

> Walter Benjamin's thought is best grasped as an allegorical one. . . .[9]

And

> Benjamin's fascination with the role of inventions in history
> seems to me most comprehensible in psychological or aesthetic
> terms.[10]

Regardless of their intent, such pronouncements function as devi-
ance-labelling, dispelling the possibility of a rigorous reading of the
argument in its own terms. Terms which stand in sharp contrast to
a conclusion such as Hannah Arendt's:

> When Adorno criticized Benjamin's "wide-eyed presentation of
> actualities". . ., he hit the nail right on its head; this is precisely what
> Benjamin was doing and wanted to do.[11]

To some extent, an understanding of this multiple-occultation
must rest on Benjamin's attitude toward the notions of super- and
substructure and the interior nature of this transformation "which
takes place far more slowly." The term *superstructure* first occurs in
the writings of Marx in *The Eighteenth Brumaire of Louis
Bonaparte* (1851–2), in a discussion of the inability of the "two
great factions of the party of Order"[12] to unite around a single
monarchical expression:

> What kept the two factions apart . . . was not any so-called
> principles, it was their material conditions of existence, two
> different kinds of property, it was the old contrast between town and
> country, the rivalry between capital and landed property. That at the
> same time old memories, personal enmities, fears and hopes,
> prejudices and illusions, sympathies and antipathies, convictions,
> articles of faith and principles bound them to one or the other royal
> house, who can deny this? Upon the different forms of property,

upon the social conditions of existence, rises an entire superstructure of distinct and peculiarly formed sentiments, illusions, modes of thought and views of life. The entire class creates and forms them out of its material foundations and out of the corresponding social relations. The single individual, who derives them through tradition and upbringing, may imagine that they form the real motives and the starting point of his activity.[13]

A quotation more often considered to be the origin of a theory of superstructure comes from the 1859 preface to *A Contribution to the Critique of Political Economy:*

In the social production of their life, men (*sic*) enter into definite relations that are indispensible and independent of their will, relations of production which correspond to a definite stage of development of their material productive forces. The sum total of these relations of production constitutes the economic structure of society, the real foundation, on which rises a legal and political superstructure and to which correspond definite forms of social consciousness. The mode of production of material life conditions the social, political and intellectual life process in general. It is not the consciousness of men that determines their being, but, on the contrary, their social being that determines their consciousness.[14]

These definitions, as Raymond Williams has noted, are not identical. *Critique* places a narrowly-defined superstructure mechanistically and unilaterally at the service of the economic realm, while the *Brumaire* acknowledges *and incorporates* into its account the transforming mediations that occur within any complex culture.

Two aspects of Benjamin's version of superstructure theory point decisively toward the earlier, dialectical formulation offered in the *Brumaire*. The more visible of these is the nature of his subject matter itself, the art work, which under the later definition would not be an element of the superstructure, but a consequence of it. Also important is the question of the "transformation . . . which takes place far more slowly than that of the substructure." This is because the "single individual . . . derives them through tradition and upbringing," conditioned by the past through education.

To a greater or lesser degree, what is learned transmits information concerning the social (and other, including the technical) conditions of some previous epoch. The highschool student who reads *Sons and Lovers* does not get an accurate portrayal of either capitalism or personal life as they exist *today*. Similarly, the model of the structure of the atom as a kind of miniature solar system has not been reputable among physicists since prior to World War I. Social being determines consciousness, but not without a detour, a gap between practice and knowledge that always renders some portion of the current moment unintelligible. On occasion this phenomenon inscribes a tangible mark in conditions as commonplace as "the generation gap," but elsewhere its unseen hand exercises a shaping grip.

This complex relation between social fact and knowledge, combined with the qualitative transformation of capitalism from the entrepreneurial stage to the imperial one, is the governing presumption of "The Work of Art."

Benjamin's position is that very little, if anything, is as it seems, but that, if subjected with caution to a particular critical process, the unspoken inner-nature can be unearthed. To do so demands not only a traditional aesthetic (or what we might now call "semiotic") analysis, but one which views the analysand in a context determined not only by the relationships of production, but also conditioned in practice by a trailing, outmoded understanding. This strongly echoes Marx' own assumptions on commodity fetishism and the "characters" of money:

> Man's reflections on the forms of social life, and consequently, also, his scientific analysis of these forms, take a course directly opposite to that of their actual historical development. He begins, post festum, with the results of the process of development ready to hand before him. The characters that stamp products as commodities, and whose establishment is a necessary preliminary to the circulation of commodities, have already acquired the stability of natural, self-understood forms of social life, before man seeks to decipher, not their historical character, for in his eyes they are immutable, but their meaning.[15]

This concept of a barrier, or fetish, hiding or inverting the meaning of concrete acts shares its central feature with both the Freudian division between conscious and unconscious, and the structuralist distinction between surface and deep phenomena[16]. It was Benjamin's accomplishment (half-hidden by his own periodic manifestations of precisely this condition) to grasp this effacement of the actual as the essential point of departure.

The third major assertion of the preface, that "theses about the developmental tendencies of art under present conditions of production"[17] should take priority over those as to the nature of cultural work in a post-revolutionary or classless society, follows as the conclusion of a syllogism:

> if Marx's critique of the capitalist mode of production occurred when that mode was in its infancy (and, having matured, is now changed), and
>
> if there exists an inevitable gap between transformations within an economic infrastructure and their mediated expressions within a broadly cultural superstructure,
>
> then delineations of the shapes art might adopt under a postulated utopia (e.g., "socialist realism") are projections grounded in a misunderstood present.

It follows that the more basic task confronting a Marxist is to investigate the present, leading from its opaque-but-visible symptoms back toward a more accurate comprehension of the underlying dynamics of the economic motor governing (however indirectly) society. Thus, in the name of their own methodology, Benjamin aligns himself in opposition to the majority of Marxist literary critics of his time. Significantly, his argument is silent on the possibility that "present conditions" might include a society in which the proletariat, or at minimum its vanguard, has already assumed power.

Having marked out such critical notions in the space of two paragraphs, Benjamin wades into the subject proper, attempting to extract in two dozen pages the numerous possible meanings contained in the phrase "The Work of Art in the Age of Mechanical Reproduction." Nearly every paragraph is a conceivable abstract for an infinitely longer writing, presenting several ideas in such emblematic form that the connotations generated enter into a kind of free play which is beyond the governability of the text.

In the first section of the piece, Benjamin states his thesis in these terms:

> In principle a work of art has always been reproducible. . . . Mechanical reproduction of a work, however, represents something new. . . . .[18]

—then sketching out the processes through which various arts have evolved to the capacity for multiple copies: founding, stamping, printing, etching, engraving, lithography, photography and finally film. He cautiously avoids getting into a detailed account of the historic role of printing, "merely a special, though particularly important case,"[19] giving greater weight to lithography, which "enabled graphic art to illustrate everyday life."[20] Benjamin focuses on the impact of photography:

> For the first time in the process of pictorial reproduction, photography freed the hand of the most important artistic functions which henceforth devolved only upon the eye looking into a lens. Since the eye perceives more swiftly than the hand can draw, the process of pictorial reproduction was accelerated so enormously that it could keep pace with speech.[21]

Without warning, the word "reproduction" has altered its definition. Before, it meant to make a copy of an (art) object, the capacity for multiplicity as such, but here it stands instead for the mimetic function of re/presenting the world through what may or may not be an aesthetic procedure.

Beyond establishing this perhaps deliberate ambiguity, Benjamin permits his description to be conditioned by precisely the kind of "tradition and upbringing" that would seem to retard an understanding of the superstructure. Photography is not viewed as a new medium, carrying within itself wholly original capacities for new modes of perception and activity, but as the next, although vital, step "in the process of pictorial reproduction." Situating the camera into this historical, teleological context is not without its rationale, however, for this was in fact how Daguerre's exposure of iodized silver plates in a camera obscura was conceived of at the very instant of its discovery. By 1840, only three years after its invention, "most of the innumerable painters of miniatures [i.e., portraits] had become professional photographers, at first only on the side, but soon, however, exclusively."[22]

If Benjamin's characterization of the photograph follows the conceptual (contextual) imprisonment into which it historically was born, it serves also to note the role of the camera in a crucial step toward the fetishized realism which embodies the capitalist mode of thought, for the hand is hardly "freed . . . of the most important artistic function," since it is the hand and nothing else which must now operate this new equipment. Instead, the hand, in the process of pictorial reproduction, is stripped of its gestural function. The obliteration of the gestural through the elaboration of technology occurs across the entire range of cultural phenomena in the capitalist period. It is the principle affective transformation of the new material basis of production. Gutenberg's moveable type erased gesturality from the graphemic dimension of books. That this in turn functions to alienate the producer from his or her product is tangible even to authors who compose on the typewriter: to see one's text in a new typeface (inevitably asserting different spatio-visual values) is almost as radical a shock as first seeing oneself on film or videotape, or initially hearing one's voice remarkably *other* on audio tape. In a parallel manner, the constantly evolving and always unique objects of master craftsmen were replaced by the uniform, infinitely reproducible, objects of mass production (where, as Benjamin was to discover, the gestural is replaced by its antithesis, style, the trace of the individual supplanted by the uniform "trademark" that expresses corporate personality: it is ironic that the Motion Picture Academy in 1978 awarded an Oscar to the inventors of the Steadicam, a new portable camera which henceforth banishes the gestural from even handheld film, a method which had previously acknowledged just this aspect as its primary virtue). Implicit within Benjamin's curious assertion that "photography freed the hand" is the discovery of that surrogate for the human spine and legs, the tripod.

Benjamin carefully skirts a direct equation between the camera and the eye. Reduced to a mechanical function, the hand yields its artistic capacity to the "eye looking into a lens," the result of which was an enormous acceleration of pictorial reproduction, because "the eye perceives more swiftly than the hand can draw." Yet it is not a seeing hand that determines which strokes to make where. Mimetic representation demands perception, organization and delivery. A line drawing reflects the process of organizing information and translating it into voluntary action. The camera, however, lacks the capacity to omit or add detail except on an all-or-nothing basis through filters, although this can be achieved later in the dark room. In the camera, the action of self-correction is reduced to one of focus. The image produced by the naive camera staring uncritically at the world is not equal to the human field of vision, but only that small part of it in focus at any given moment. The human eye is continually scanning its environment through a series of rapid, discontinuous refocusings. At the edge of the visual field color perception declines greatly. These refocusings, as well as the commonly recognized problems of miniaturization and loss of depth perception, radically separate the photograph from sight, although sight is the sole means available for experiencing the photograph. For 140 years the photograph has been educating sight in the industrial nations (a phenomenon which reaches a sad apotheosis in the film buff who lives each moment of life as though it were a "shot").

Only Benjamin's irrepressible urge to tell everything in the shortest possible time enables him to argue that "the process of pictorial reproduction was accelerated so enormously that it could keep pace with speech." He himself had written, five years earlier, that "The lower sensitivity to light of the early plates made necessary a long period of exposure in the open."[23] But the gist is clear enough. The inevitability of motion pictures was inscribed entirely within the first still daguerreotype. Likewise, the successful production of sound recordings in the late 1870s made the marriage of sound to film a *fait accompli*, although one which took 50 years to consummate. "Around 1900," Benjamin writes, restating his thesis with a new sense of focus,

> technical reproduction had reached a standard that not only permitted it to reproduce all transmitted works of art and thus to cause the most profound change in their impact upon the public; it also had captured a place of its own among the artistic processes.[24]

By now, it is evident that Benjamin's concern in "The Work of Art" is with at least three interlocking problems: (1) changes in the art object as object; (2) the transformation of mimetic representation; (3) reproducibility as an aesthetic process. Having established something approximating a foundation on which to develop these concerns, Benjamin shifts tone and mode in the next section. Instead of rattling off the names of media to illustrate a space of more than two thousand years in two paragraphs, the text is suddenly all but devoid of examples. In contrast, it introduces theoretical terms rapidly and without extensive definition, from *presence* through *authenticity, authority* and *aura*, to *tradition*:

> Even the most perfect reproduction of a work of art is lacking in one element: its presence in time and space, its unique existence at the place where it happens to be. . . .
>
> The presence of the original is the prerequisite to the concept of authenticity. . . . the quality of its presence is always depreciated. . . . The authenticity of a thing is the essence of all that is transmissable from its beginning. . . . what is really jeopardized . . . is the authority of the object.
>
> One might subsume the eliminated element in the term "aura" and go on to say: that which withers in the age of mechanical reproduction is the aura of the work of art. . . . the technique of reproduction detaches the reproduced object from the domain of tradition.[25]

The term which governs this sequence, *lacking* anticipates the work of Jacques Derrida. The problem of mechanical reproduction is one of the metaphysics of presence itself. "Essence is presence," Derrida has written.[26] Yet, just as the definition of any word is the sum of those denotation and connotations not specifically excluded, presence is knowable only in the face of a possible absence. Absence, a lacking, is *not only* a precondition for presence: neither can ever occur without implying the other. Thus writing (which Derrida, following Rousseau, defines as the death of speech, since there language loses its voice (presence)) was required for the origin of speech in the first place. Hence writing precedes speech and contains it, or so Derrida presumes to have demonstrated in *Of Grammatology*. Yet writing was also a reproduction of speech, at first manual, later technical. Writing adds to speech because speech has a lack, which is the pre-existence of writing. Writing is a supplement. Unlike manual reproduction, which is considered plagiarized and a forgery, mechanical reproduction, for Benjamin, is likewise a supplement:

> The reason is twofold. First, process reproduction is more independent of the original. . . . For example, in photography, process reproduction can bring out those aspects of the original that are unattainable to the naked eye yet accessible to the lens. . . . photographic reproduction . . . can capture images which escape natural vision. Secondly, technical reproduction can put the copy . . .

into situations which would be out of reach for the original itself. Above all, it enables the original to meet the beholder halfway, be it in the form of a photograph or a phonograph record.[27]

What the reproduced art object is lacking is *presence* because, through reproduction, presence is *depreciated* and the resulting object's authority jeopardized: "One might subsume the eliminated element in the term 'aura' and go on to say: that which withers in the age of mechanical reproduction is the aura of the work of art." In the next section of the essay, Benjamin writes:

> The concept of the aura which was proposed above with reference to historical objects may be usefully defined with reference to the aura of natural ones. We define the aura of the latter as *the unique phenomenon of a distance*, however close it may be. If, while resting on a summer afternoon, you follow with your eyes a mountain range on the horizon or a branch which casts its shadow over you, you experience the aura of those mountains, of that branch.[28]

A definition and an example, neither of which are explicit as to the cause and nature of this "phenomenon of a distance." Nor is this distance in the physical sense, since the object experienced may or may not be "close." These sentences revise only slightly what Benjamin had written in the "Short History of Photography":

> What is aura? *A strange web of time and space:* the unique appearance of a distance, however close at hand. On a summer noon, resting, to follow the line of a mountain range on the horizon or a twig which throws its shadow on the observer, *until the moment or hour begins to be a part of its appearance*—that is to breathe the aura of those mountains, that twig.[29]

The eleventh section of "On Some Motifs in Baudelaire" is also devoted to a discussion of aura, both that which Benjamin discerns in the French poet's verse and, again, in the daguerreotype, which Baudelaire is said to have found "profoundly unnerving and terrifying."[30] There, aura is defined rather differently:

> If we designate as aura the associations which, at home in the *mémoire involontaire*, tend to cluster around the object of a

perception, then its analogue in the case of a utilitarian object is the experience which has left traces of the practiced hand.[31]

Experience of the aura . . . rests on thè transposition of a response common in human relationships to the relationship between the inanimate or natural object and man. The person we look at or who feels he is being looked at, looks at us in turn. To perceive the aura of an object we look at means to invest it with the ability to look at us in return. This experience corresponds to the data of the *mémoire involuntaire*. (These data . . . are lost to the memory that seeks to retain them. . . .)[32]

In a note to this last passage, Benjamin quotes Karl Kraus: "The closer the look one takes at a word, the greater the distance from which it looks back."[33] The dialectic is exact.

These definitions occupy a territory between *presence* and *intersubjectivity* without ever being identical with either. There is a gradual shift from the first formulation in the "History," which speaks of aura as exterior ("web of time and space"), and a quality ("the moment or hour begins to be a part of its appearance"), to the later one of the "Motifs," in which aura is invested or injected by the viewer's perception. Although this shift signals the deepening analysis of this issue, which is the focal point of Benjamin's work, it should not obscure the fundamental thrust which these definitions share. Appearance, which is specifically an object *in relation* to an observer, is in each instance the privileged notion. Under the name of aura what appears is the Other, a shock, the recognition and acknowledgement of its absolute integrity freed from any dependency on the presence of Self. This liberty presents itself as "distance" and "the experience which has left traces of the practiced hand." It does not (cannot) occur abstractly, in the absence of the concrete object *as presence*. This is how aura escapes both memory and reproduction. The affective presence of a photograph of a massacre, a Rembrandt or an orchid, is first of all that of a (gray) rectangle of a certain size, which is almost never the dimension of the event or object portrayed.

What is radically new in the age of technical reproduction is the increased value placed on the possession of entities which have been deprived of their integrity and otherness, personal experience reduced to vicarious consumption. But to lose the Other is, in the same instant, to abandon one's sense of Self, without which

45

intersubjectivity is not possible. One is rendered numb and passive on a level not previously feasible in history. In "The Work of Art," Benjamin defines aura by exposing its "decay," its very existence revealed by its lack in mechanical reproduction, and goes further to implicate as the origin of this erosion not merely industrial imperialism, but that which made capitalism itself (and even capital) possible, the constituting myth of western civilization, *Identity*. This section begins with a cautious paraphrase of the being-determines-consciousness preface to *Critique of Political Economy*

> And if changes in the medium of contemporary perception can be comprehended as decay of the aura, it is possible to show its social causes.[34]

These are:

> the desire of contemporary masses to bring things "closer" spatially and humanly which is just as ardent as their bent toward overcoming the uniqueness of every reality by accepting its reproduction.[35]

But these desires are not so much "causes" or "bases" as they are aspects. What is required is an understanding of how these desires come into existence. Noting that the gratification of each is found in the technically reproduced artifact, Benjamin makes a simple assertion whose bald outrageousness, in the frame of the 1930s, can never be fully recaptured in the light of its now "self-evident" character. The first word is precisely that type of cautionary term used defensively in order to divert the reader's reflection from the fact that, in most cases, it was just the reverse which was commonly believed to have been true:

> Unmistakably, reproduction as offered by picture magazines and newsreels differs from the image seen by the unarmed eye.[36]

The difference is one of aura. "Uniqueness and permanence," evidence of its presence, "are as closely linked" in the unmediated image as is their opposite, its absence, in the reproduction:

> To pry an object from its shell, to destroy its aura, is the mark of a perception whose "sense of the universal equality of things" has

increased to such a degree that it extracts it even from a unique object by means of reproduction.[37]

A "sense of the universal equality of things," equivalence, destroys aura by the removal of the object from its constituting context. This is also its advantage, since concealed within it is the whole of the scientific method and project. Identity, the prerequisite for equivalence, is $A = A$, $A = -A$. The application of the process is not restricted to the mathematical mode of knowledge: contemporary philosophy begins with the first sentence of Wittgenstein's *Tractatus*: "The world is all that is the case."[38] Each of the five fundamental axioms of Euclidean geometry, which served for centuries as the model for science itself, is in some sense a statement of equivalence, of which the first is "Things equal to the same thing are equal to each other"[39] (If $A = B$ and $B = C$, then $A = C$, etc.). Thus equivalence begets substitution, exchange, reproduction. This principle extends itself into the economic sphere via the *universal equivalent* of money. Anticipating Benjamin, Marx writes of this in *Capital* in the section concerning the fetishism of commodities:

> when we bring the products of our labour into relation with each other as values, it is not because we see in these articles the material receptacles of homogeneous human labour. Quite the contrary; whenever, by an exchange, we equate as values our different products, by that very act, we also equate, as human labour, the different kinds of labour expended upon them. We are not aware of this, nevertheless we do it. Value, therefore, does not stalk about with a label describing what it is. It is value, rather, that converts every product into a social hieroglyphic. Later on, we try to decipher the hieroglyphic, to get behind the secret of our own social products; for to stamp an object of utility as a value, is just as much a social product as language. . . . It is, however, just this ultimate money form of the world of commodities that actually conceals, instead of disclosing, the social character of private labour, and the social relations between the individual producers. When I state that coats or boots stand in relation to linen, because it is the universal incarnation of abstract human labour, the absurdity of the statement is self-evident. Nevertheless, when the producers of coats and boots compare those articles with linen, or, what is the same thing with gold or silver, as the universal equivalent, they express the relation between their own private labour and the collective labour of society in the same absurd form.[40]

What Benjamin saw emerging from the iodized silver plates of Daguerre was the decisive moment in which the social basis of reality was transformed. Where previously the manufactured objects of the world submitted themselves to the fetishizing and mutational laws of identity and exchange solely through an economic process, they now did so on a new level, that of information. Each such product must not only carry on a second life as a commodity, but a third one as an image or "datum." This overdetermination of the object is not dissolved by noting that information enters into, and is supportive of, the capitalist mode of production: images rupture need from demand, implanting desire in the place of necessity. Doubly obscured, these products of the so-called communications industry organize the normative social reality of contemporary life. Film, sound recording, radio, television and the numerous other media of the "consciousness" business extend the leap forward, continually reorganizing the internal structure of the industry itself through technological innovation. Still photography has now been pushed to the periphery, but no development has as yet gone beyond reproduction and (what is the same thing) transmission at a distance.

The effect of the reproduction of an object, Benjamin insists, is "to destroy its aura." He does not argue, as McLuhan might, that a new aura comes into existence, that of the copy as a formal entity, as an object in itself. This position, although not explicitly developed in "The Work of Art," is consistent with both Benjamin's stance towards superstructure and the privilege he gives to fetishism. If, in fact, mechanical reproductions do possess auras beyond those, inevitably decayed, of their content, "tradition and upbringing" educate the observer against the recognition of their presence. This is what Roland Barthes means when he writes of "the special status of the photographic image: *it is a message without a code.*"[41] The presence of aura even in reproduction is also what enables Sartre to anticipate the Walkman in the statement which heads this essay: one can never listen to recorded music or speech without, in the same instant, hearing the mode of transmission, a supplement of electricity, that which effaces the aura. This is readily apparent in less expensive sound systems, but it never entirely recedes, even with the contemporary compact disk.

But Benjamin's position contains a problem, the question of art, for if the aura "of a utilitarian object is the experience which has left traces of the practiced hand," is this same element of style not the determiner of aura in the aesthetic object, even if, as is sometimes the case, the work in question is a photograph? He approaches this issue with another of his lightning-quick sequences of tightly compacted theories, in which key points appear in the notes as well as the body of the text. The model for Benjamin's construction is Marx's distinction between use and exchange value. For Benjamin, the use value of art was originally to be found in its ritual or cult functions. In one of the finest leaps of insight in "The Work of Art," he notes (literally) that the unapproachability of a ritual object coincides with his definition of aura as "the unique phenomenon of a distance, however close it may be." Benjamin points to the hegemony of "the secular cult of beauty"[42] as the cause of the erosion of use value in art:

> for the first time in world history, mechanical reproduction emancipates the work of art from its parasitical dependence on ritual. To an ever greater degree the work of art reproduced becomes the work of art designed for reproducibility. From a photographic negative, for example, one can make any number of prints; to ask for the "authentic" print makes no sense. But the instant the criterion of authenticity ceases to be applicable to artistic production, the total function of art is reversed. Instead of being based on ritual, it begins to be based on another practice—politics.[43]

Politics, it turns out, means economics, use subordinated to exchange, until in "photography, exhibition value begins to displace cult value all along the line."[44] But the emancipation is incomplete and cult value is perpetuated in "an ultimate retrenchment," the form of the portrait.

In the portrait Benjamin sees the last flicker of aura, but at best it is a fetishism born of nostalgia: the first photographs of people mimicked miniature portrait painting in their exclusion of most background detail because of the limited sensitivity of the plates to light. When, 40 years hence, the chemistry of the process had advanced to eliminate the formal necessity for this halo-like effect, photographers sought to restore it through retouching. Of this, Benjamin had written in the "Short History,"

> The conquest of darkness by increased illumination had eliminated the aura from the picture as thoroughly as the increasing alienation

of the imperialist bourgeoisie had eliminated it from reality.[45]

Nowhere, perhaps, is the evolution of Benjamin's thought over the five years between these two pieces toward a more fully dialectical position more clear. The militance of that earlier language is in sharp contrast to that of "The Work of Art," where, following the calculated reversal to a positive terminology begun two pages before with the "emancipation" passage, he writes that

> as man withdraws from the photographic image, the exhibition value for the first time shows its superiority to the ritual value. To have pinpointed this new stage constitutes the incomparable significance of Atget, who, around 1900, took photographs of deserted Paris streets.[46]

Yet Atget was neither the first photographer to purge "man" from his images, nor the most extreme: William Henry Fox Talbot had been making "direct contact reproductions of prints, drawing, lace and leaf forms in the late 1850s."[47] The photogram, which Talbot's "photogenic drawings" anticipate, reveals by its opposition the extent to which the "natural" capacities of the "innocent" photo reflect culturally determined attitudes toward the "inherent" laws of art. Roland Barthes, in a passage quoted in part earlier, presents a capsule semiology of what might, following Thomas Kuhn, be called normal photography:

> What is the content of the photographic message? What does the photograph transmit? By definition, the scene itself, the literal reality. From the object to its image there is of course a reduction— in proportion, perspective, colour—but at no time is this reduction a *transformation* (in the mathematical sense of the term). In order to move from the reality to its photograph it is in no way necessary to divide up this reality into units and to constitute these units as signs, substantially different from the object they communicate; there is no necessity to set up a relay, that is to say a code, between the object and its image. Certainly the image is not the reality but it is its perfect *analogon* and it is exactly this analogical perfection which, to common sense, defines the photograph. Thus can be seen the special status of the photographic image: *it is a message without a code*; from which proposition an important corollary must immediately be drawn: the photographic message is a continuous message.[48]

But art, an aesthetic relay, is just such a code (which Barthes himself later concedes). The achievement of Atget, who seems not to have considered himself an artist and certainly did not treat his pictures as valuable aesthetic objects, is thus an absolute division between form and content. Form, which exists in the naive or "realist" photograph as selection and framing (and elsewhere as any conscious manipulation, either of subject, camera, negative or print), situates the finished product within the code of art. This code is one of exchange in which value is structured precisely upon an historic elaboration of formal elements or styles. Thus any print by Robert Frank is wedded to a history that invokes (and ranks) the name and art of Walker Evans. A similar relationship, as Barthes elaborates on in *Camera Lucida*, can be found between Nadar, Sander, Avedon and Mapplethorpe. In Atget, content recedes dramatically to the point where it exists merely as an incidental signal in the code of form: what made his street scenes art was the fact that he photographed the same type of subject consistently, permitting the structural message of his framing technique to become visible.

The polar opposite of normal photography is the photogram, discovered independently twice between the years 1920 and '22, after numerous anticipations, such as Talbot's, by Man Ray and Laszlo Moholy-Nagy, both modernist artists active in several media, particularly painting. Man Ray, who supported himself as a portrait photographer, felt the camera had liberated painting from the grip of representation. In fact, he at one time held photography not to be an art at all. Nevertheless, when an unexposed sheet of paper fell accidentally into his developing tray, he had the insight to place "the funnel, graduate and thermometer in the tray on the wetted paper"[49] and turn on the light until an image, or what might more accurately be termed a text, appeared. In contrast, Moholy-Nagy was actively looking for a mode that would register light as such, rather than the "look of light" on things.[50] He was working with photomontage, itself a recently identified practice, when he too arrived at what he named the photogram. In the work of these modernists,

> The photogram produces space without existing spatial structure only by articulation on the plane of the paper with the advancing and receding values of half-tones in black and gray and

with the power of their contrasts and gradations. Through this elimination of pigment and texture the photogram achieves a dematerialized effect. It is a writing and drawing with light, self-expressive through the contrasting relationships of black, white and gray.[51]

In short, nothing exists in the photogram which is not transformed into a consciously formal element, nothing which does not enter into the code of visual aesthetics, in which its message is precisely its *place* within the history of aesthetic values, the social narrative of forms. Moholy-Nagy himself treated the photogram as if it were a direct descendant of constructivist painting, although Man Ray's practice is more clearly in the cubist tradition.

This is the decisive moment of origin for all abstract or formal modes of photography, including such recent extensions as structuralist cinema. Defining light, and not the camera, as the irreducible element, the photogram proposed a reversal in the usual relation of content to form in which the aura itself might be resurrected. If, when practiced as art, normal photography reduced content to background information, formalist strategies, by definition, made form itself the basis of a possible content. *But—* the trap to which this promise instantly submits itself is idealism, since it presumes feasible an absolute break between these two poles which does not, and cannot, in concrete practice, exist: each infiltrates and undermines the other. If the hidden question in a realist picture, be it Atget's or Robert Frank's, is *What is the form?* that of the painterly text of the formalist photo is *How was this taken?*, a question which barely disguises *What is this picture of, what is the content?*

The problem of content penetrated the photogram (and all abstract photography) at its very beginning. Many of Man Ray's photograms are "portraits" of the object's manipulation of light. It was soon understood that negatives of "normal scenes" could similarly be altered by this darkroom process, an effect almost identical in spirit with certain aspects of surrealism, such as the "melting" watches of Salvador Dali. A like infiltration in the opposite direction can be found in the works of the late Diane Arbus: grotesque content offers the possibility of content, as such, *de*formed not through a medium of art, but by life itself. That stylization which, in art, is the mark of form's presence (the shadow of the hand of the creator) is seen, once it is imposed on the individual, some hapless cultural or physical mutant, as the sign of life's sheer otherness, aura reduced to horror.

Most art photography exists as a compromise between those polar opposites. In the gay semiology of Hal Fisher, homosexual males are photographed in poses consciously reminiscent of fashion advertising. Beyond this ironic framing device, the role of the camera itself is neutral. Specific elements of gay dress, related to the social functioning of homosexual lifestyle in pre-AIDS America, are labelled. The labels, characteristic of the '70s chic conjunction of images with words in all the visual arts, establishes Fisher's work within an aesthetic code, even more strongly than either the framing or consistency of subject matter. What the words actually signify is their own supplementarity, the super-imposition of a code (art) onto a passive content.

The inevitable penetration of one dimension into the other prohibits photography, as it does any art based on the possibility of reference (i.e., the coexistence of form and content), from resurrecting a true aura. At best, in the most militant extremes of formalism or realism aura appears as both memory and promise. Marcuse has written in depth on the role of memory as revolutionary instinct. Just as art, however limited or compromised, offers society an image of the possibility of unalienated labor, memory, recalling that once things were different (needs were met), poses the possibility that things might change, or that change itself has the potential to exist. Indeed, for Marcuse,

> The memory of gratification is at the origin of all thinking, and the impulse to recapture past gratification is the hidden driving power behind the process of thought.[52]

The memory of aura, that shock of the presence of the Other without which intersubjectivity cannot exist, and thus cannot invoke a recognition of one's own self-presence, is thereby a fundamentally revolutionary instinct. The memory of a lost or debased aura may, in fact, be more powerful and critical than the fact of aura itself. It is here, then, that we must place, and re-evaluate, the function of what many critics have described as Benjamin's nostalgia.

"The Work of Art" itself continues through a more leisurely

examination of the film industry, followed by a discussion of the role of distraction versus that of concentration in art viewing, and a final reassertion of the political presumptions of the essay. While one might quarrel with certain relatively minor points (such as the fact that it is not the mass audience which owns the motion picture: they may purchase it as a commodity with their ticket, only to have it vanish (back) into an (advertising) image the instant they leave the theater, but it is the producer, finally, who owns the product; or that video and not cinema is the prototype of an art medium based on distraction, though Benjamin could not have been expected to have foreseen *MTV* in 1936), the soundness of what follows is evident enough. It is in these first pages leading into the decisive moment of the discovery of photography where Benjamin sketches forth an aesthetic theory simultaneously Marxist and in anticipation of structuralism, without many of the limitations often associated with either. Realism and formalism in photography are both predicated on a "past understanding," the model of painting. In this sense all photography is problematic:

> With the different methods of technical reproduction of a work of art, its fitness for exhibition increased to such an extent that the quantitative shift between its two poles turned into a qualitative transformation of its nature. This is comparable to the situation of the work of art in prehistoric times when, by the absolute emphasis on its cult value, it was, first and foremost, an instrument of magic. Only later did it become recognized as a work of art. In the same way today, by the absolute emphasis on its exhibition value the work of art becomes a creation with entirely new functions, among which the one we are conscious of, the artistic function, later may be recognized as incidental. This much is certain: today photography and the film are the most serviceable exemplifications of this new function.[53]

It is through the decline and loss of aura that modern humanity affectively confronts the myth of identity and equivalence, the myth of exchange within which capitalism itself is inscribed. Benjamin was the first to recognize this confrontation, which further explains his reversal from a negative to a positive terminology to describe the "emancipation" of the object, the liberation of the signifier from its signified: within this movement, however hidden and mute, must lie the seeds of any future transformation of humankind.

II ～～～～～

For $L = A = N = G = U = A = G = E$

Word's a sentence before it's a word—I write sentences— When words are, meaning soon follows—Where words join, writing is—One's writing is one writing—Not all letters are equal—2 phrases yield an angle—Eye settles in the middle of word, left of center—Reference is a compass—Each day—Performance seeks vaudeville—Composition as investigation—Collage is a false democracy—Spelling's choices—Line defined by its closure: the function is nostalgic—Nothing without necessity—By hand— Individuals do not exist—Keep mind from sliding—Structure is metaphor, content permission, syntax force—Don't imitate yourself—We learned the language—Aesthetic consistency = voice—How does a work end?

OF THEORY, TO PRACTICE

> To write poetry after Auschwitz is
> barbaric.
> —Theodor Adorno

Lenin's comment that "Thought, rising from the concrete to the abstract, does not get farther away *from* the truth, but gets closer to it"[1] stands in sharp contrast to the stated beliefs of many, perhaps most, 20th century American poets, expressed succinctly by Williams' "no ideas but in things." Such a self-containment would seem to preclude any "rising from the concrete to the abstract." Robert Creeley states the case for this confinement:

> A poetry denies its end in any *descriptive* act, I mean any act which leaves its attention outside the poem. Our anger cannot exist usefully without its objects, but a description of them is also a perpetuation. There is that confusion—one wants the thing to act on, and yet hates it. *Description* does nothing, it includes the object—it neither hates nor loves.[2]

He carries this to a logical conclusion, one that apparently manifests itself in the early poems of Clark Coolidge: "poems are not referential, or at least not importantly so."[3]

Yet the work of both Creeley and Williams is actively concerned with theory. *Words, Pieces* and *Spring & All* explicitly address issues of writing without ceasing to be literature. Both poets have written reviews, theoretical essays and prefaces. Each has been associated with at least one semi-organized literary movement. If a contradiction is perceived between their practice and their discourse about it, this is due only to a misconception of the function of theory, and to the sort of degeneration which occurs when any idea is generalized through popular usage (such as that which has rendered "no ideas but in things" the battle cry of anti-intellectualism in verse).

The goal of poetry can never be the proof of theory, although it is inevitably a test of the poet's beliefs. Such beliefs are themselves the writer's perceptions of *already-written* poems (by others as well as oneself), combined with a sense of a desired direction: "this is where I want my poem to go."

Not surprisingly for a society based on capitalism and its ideology of individualism, these perceptions often consist of unorganized intuitions. Intuition is, for me, the critical term in this discussion. It is the raw material of what Lukács terms "proletarian consciousness." In its unorganized state, it can only *react* "spontaneously" to the undigested phenomenological data of everyday life. Reaction, in this sense, is always the inverse of action: it is the kind of intuition that recognizes the objective existence of a large mass of permanently unemployed black males in this society, without perceiving why or how such a fact has come to be, thus apt to blame individuals for a lifestyle they were born and literally tracked into. Organized intuition would transfer one's anger to the appropriate causes of this condition. One rises from the concrete person to the abstract politics of labor.

This has everything to do with poetry, but not in the way of justifying propaganda. The writer cannot organize her desires for writing without some vision of the world toward which one hopes to work, and without having some concept of how literature might participate in such a future. Unorganized reactive intuition is incapable of achieving any vision beyond the current fact, although it is quite able to psychologically block much of what makes the present unpleasant. Dozens of happy love poems are written every day.

As the organization of intuition and critical perception, theory functions in poetic practice through the selection of goals and strategies. This specifically implies the *rejection* of some in favor of others. To the degree that these methods differ visibly from those of the past (a shift which may rightly be interpreted as a rejection of the present), their result will be works of art which appear new.

The production of novelty, of art objects that could not have been predicted, and cannot be accounted for, by previous critical theory, is the most problematic area in aesthetics. Like a record in sports, made only to be broken, a poetics is articulated in order to be transcended.

Yet there is something about American poetry in the 20th century which is generating an increasingly rapid evolution of form(s). The formal distance between Dryden and Yeats is less than between Pound and Watten. Just as *Personae* now reeks of an epoch from which it was once thought to be a radical break, any poet writing today is assured a future conventionality beyond their control. No doubt the pressure of this acceleration in literary historicity contributes to confusion, doubt and defensiveness on the part of poets and likewise sets the stage for works whose sole redeeming value is some vague commitment to Make It Different, if not new.

Heretofore, discussion of this "heating up" of forms has been in the terms of commodification, which seems generally correct, as far as it goes. But poetry is only partly a commodity in the strict sense of that term, in that to become a commodity a product must specifically be created with the purpose of exchange within a market. All books and magazines are commodities, but not all poems, a fact which complicates literature, creating numerous levels of bastard cases.

There is, however, a second factor, one first noted by Laura Riding,[4] contributing to this disease of newness in poetics, related to the poem as product, not commodity. This is a shift in perception of the role of form in modern life, specifically as an *index of labor*. The more any product looks like its predecessors, the less work appears to have gone into it.

This is true for many cases. The less modification one must make from one generation of a product to the next, the less capital an owner, corporate or otherwise, must expend in design and "modernization" of manufacturing equipment. The capitalist is thus permitted to either carry these unexpended costs forward in the price of the product as pure surplus value, or else to amortize them over a longer period of time, lowering the price in order to expand the potential market. Consider the history of the Volkswagen "bug."

An object's life as product is fused with its career as

commodity. The origin of style, as Riding sensed and Walter Benjamin stated explicitly, is the transference of the perception of the *labor : form* relation away from structure towards packaging. Most automobiles just look new. So too the poem.

It is a loaded question whether less labor need be put into a sonnet than into the prosoid works of contemporary poets. Certainly the disjuncture between the regularities of the sonnet form and the discordances of contemporary life render any good one a monument of productive work. But in the case of the loosely written, speech-like free verse dramatic monolog concerning the small travails of daily existence—in short *most poems now being written*—the conclusion is painfully evident. Half of the graduate students in any creative writing program can turn these out with no more effort than it takes to bake bread.

But is labor a value in itself for poetry? Among the several social functions of poetry is that of posing a model of unalienated work: it stands in relation to the rest of society both as utopian possibility and constant reminder of just how bad things are. But here too the situation of the poem is undergoing change. Once this template of useful activity was predicated upon the image of the poem as individual craft of the artisan type, while now the collective literature of the community, an ensemble of "scenes," is gradually emerging as more vital than the production of single authors. In either situation, maximum productivity is going to be a critical quality of labor. In the poem this means a maximum of effort.

This does not mean that good poetry should, prima facie, be difficult or obscure. Modernism has been no less immune to the shift in emphasis from production to consumption than other domains of life, and much literature can be reduced to the consumption of effort, in which the opposite of difficulty is thought to be trash. *Spring & All, "A" 9* and *Pieces* might have cured us of that, but obviously they haven't. Once reading strategies catch up to those of writing, a lot of complexity is going to dissolve. Ease awes. For good reason.

All these issues have crucial analogs at the level of writing itself. For example, the recognition that the very presence of the line is the predominant current signifier of The Poetic will cause some poets to discard, at least for a time, its use. This, in turn, requires a new organizational strategy constructed around a different primary unit. Two alternative candidates have recently been proposed: (1) prose works built around investigations of the sentence (although Watten and Hejinian's approach to paragraph and stanza are interesting variations); (2) the page itself as spatial unit filled with "desyntaxed" words or phrases, as in the work of Bruce Andrews. Either road is going to determine the kinds of language which the resulting poem can incorporate and that means restricting to some degree the domains of life which can be presented.

In the *sentence-centered* poem, a major problematic surrounds the use of long sentences. Unless one is specifically seeking the ironic tonality of an Ashbery, long hypotactic sentences cannot be strung together so as to hold a reader's attention without highly convoluted internal syntax to break them down into phrase clusters. Even more difficult is the long sentence taken from a class-specific professional jargon with a minimal use of clear "technical" terms. The special, oppressive meanings of these words (an important area of language to investigate) tend to disappear when removed from originating contexts.

Andrews' *page-as-field* presents different problems. The polysemic quality of words at the bottom or top of the paper is lost when a work is presented on two (or more) pages. Print alters the invariant em of the typewriter. Syntax, that lineating element, also has a habit of reinserting itself in even the smallest of phrases. As Robert Grenier has shown, the organization of letters into a single word already presumes the presence of a line.

Are these examples of poetry made subservient to (or, in Creeley's words, "describing") theory? No more than the sonnet. Every mode of poem is the manifestation of some set of assumptions. It's no more foolish to be conscious of them—and their implications extending into the daily life of the real world—than it is to actually have some idea how to drive before getting behind the wheel of a car.

THE NEW SENTENCE

> To please a young man there should be
> sentences. What are sentences. Like what
> are sentences. In the part of sentences it
> for him is happily all. They will name
> sentences for him. Sentences are called
> sentences.
>
> Gertrude Stein

The sole precedent I can find for the new sentence is *Kora In Hell: Improvisations* and that one far-fetched.

I am going to make an argument, that there is such a thing as a new sentence and that it occurs thus far more or less exclusively in the prose of the Bay Area. Therefore this talk is aimed at the question of the prose poem. I say aimed because, in order to understand why so little is in fact understood about sentences and prose poems, a certain amount of background material is needed.

The proposition of a new sentence suggests a general understanding of sentences per se, against which an evolution or shift can be contrasted.

This poses a first problem. There is, in the domain of linguistics, philosophy and literary criticism, no adequate consensus at to the definition of a sentence. Odd as that seems, there are reasons for it.

Milka Ivić, in *Trends in Linguistics*, noted that linguists, by the 1930's, had proposed and were using more than 160 different definitions of "the sentence."

The word sentence is itself of relatively recent origin,

according to the OED, deriving from 12th Century French. As a noun, the OED proposes 9 definitions. Among them:

> 5) An *indefinite* portion of a discourse or writing.
> 6) A series of words in connected speech or writing, forming the grammatically complete expression of a single thought; in popular use often such a portion of a composition or utterance as extends *from one full stop to another.*

This definition dates from 1447.

Contained in the sixth definition is the notation that in grammar, a sentence is either a proposition, question, command or request, containing subject and predicate, though one of these may be absent by means of ellipsis; likewise the OED acknowledges 3 classes of sentences: simple, compound and complex, and notes that one word may be a sentence.

In the November, 1978, *Scientific American,* Breyne Arlene Moskowitz presents a summary discussion of recent developments in the theory of language acquisition in children:

> The first stage of child language is one in which the maximum sentence length is one word; it is followed by a stage in which the maximum sentence length is two words . . . By the time the child is uttering two-word sentences with some regularity, her lexicon may include hundreds of words . . . an important criterion is informativeness, that is, the child selects a word reflecting what is new in a particular situation.[1]

Here is an abbreviated conversation between a child at the one-word stage and an adult, which indicates the sentence-function of single words:

> C: Car. Car.
> A: What?
> C: Go. Go.
> A: What?
> C: Bus. Bus. Bus.
> A: Bicycle?
> C: No![2]

Even before the one-word stage, the child is playing with the babbling prosody of sentence forms which are considerably longer, until gradually the intonation contours of normal speech are acquired. This suggests that the child *hears* sentences before it can break them down into smaller units—that is, that the sentence is in some sense a primary unit of language.

The absence of a 3-word stage is also worth noting. From the 2-word stage, an infant enters the realm of sentences of variable length.

Finally, we should pay attention to the fact that Moskowitz is talking about speech, not writing, a distinction that will be getting more important.

Here is another example of speech, a telephone conversation:

E. Hello?
L. Hi Ed.
E. Hi Lisa.
L. I'm running around here trying to get my machines done [+] and I'd like to get it all done before I leave, [+] so I won't have to come back. [−] So that might push us up till near two. How is that?
E. That's fine. My only thing is that I have to leave here like around 3:15 or so.
L. 3:15. [−] OK. Let me see how I'm doing here, [+] then I'll give you a call right before I'm going to leave.
E. OK. [−] Fine.
L. Okey doke. Bye bye.
E. Bye.[3]

Ed Friedman has written this conversation up as 16 distinct sentences. There are at least 6 places in this short script that could have been transcribed differently (indicated by + or − signs inserted into the text), rendering the conversation into as few as 13 or as many as 19 sentences. There are, in fact, 64 separate ways to transcribe this conversation without radically altering the acceptibility of any of its sentences.

Which brings us to the question, not of sentences in speech, but in modern linguistics, as a discipline and tradition, normally considered as beginning with Saussure's *Course in General Linguistics*. Saussure mentions the sentence in this work on only three occasions. All take place in the second part of his course, concerning synchronic linguistics.

The first mention is in the area of locating practical delimiting units of language. Saussure is quoted as saying:

A rather widely held theory makes sentences the concrete units of language: we speak only in sentences and subsequently single out the words. But to what extent does the sentence belong to language [*langue*]? If it belongs to speaking [*parole*], the sentence cannot pass for the linguistic unit. But let us suppose this difficulty is set aside. If we picture to ourselves in their totality the sentences that could be uttered, their most striking characteristic is that in no way do they resemble each other . . . diversity is dominant, and when we look for the link that bridges their diversity, again we find, without having looked for it, the word . . . [4]

The distinction between language and speaking (*langue* and *parole*) is critical. Saussure is analyzing only one, *langue*, and by putting the sentence into the domain of the other, he removes it from the major area of his inquiry. More than any other reason, this is the origin of the failure of the modern human sciences to develop a consensus as to the definition of such a critical term.

Saussure's second mention completes the setting aside of the sentence into the realm of *parole*. It is in the section on syntagmatic relations, in the chapter which historically first divides paradigm from syntagm. The syntagmatic axis is that of connection between words, as in syntax:

. . . the notion of syntagm applies not only to words but to groups of words, to complex units of all lengths and types (compounds, derivatives, phrases, whole sentences).

It is not enough to consider the relation that ties together the different parts of syntagms, one must also bear in mind the relation that links the whole to its parts.

An objection must be raised at this point. The sentence is the ideal type of syntagm. But it belongs to speaking, not to language. [5]

The sentence has been shoved back into the domain of non-investigation, the realm of parole, but without a clear and decisive argument. These two quotations conspire without proof for the dismissal of the sentence as an object of critical investigation.

The only other area where Saussure even mentions the sentence is in the problem of one-word sentences and the question of whether or not they possess a syntagmatic dimension. The language used demonstrates the problem raised by the dismissal of sentence theory from linguistics:

> To be sure, language has independent units that have syntagmatic relations with neither their parts nor other units. Sentence equivalents like *yes, no, thanks*, etc. are good examples. But this exceptional fact does not compromise the general principle.[6]

Given this denegration at the origin of modern linguistics, it is not surprising that the sentence is neither defined nor even indexed in Louis Hjelmslev's 1943 *Prolegomena to a Theory of Language*.

In America during this same period, the most influential practicing linguist was Leonard Bloomfield, who, in *Language* (1933), defined the sentence as:

> An independent linguistic form, not included by virture of any grammatical construction in any larger form.

This definition is void of any internal criteria. The sentence is merely a limit, the point beyond which grammatical analysis cannot be further extended. In a sense this goes back to the OED definition of a sentence as being what comes between two full stops, regardless of what that might be.

One might expect a fuller treatment in Chomsky's *Aspects of the Theory of Syntax* (1965), insofar as syntax and the syntagmatic is the one area where Saussure even permits the sentence as a question to surface, and since Chomsky is working with such concepts as acceptability, deviant sentences, and kernal sentences. But he raises the issue only in the prefatory "methodological preliminaries" chapter. "I shall use the term 'sentence' to refer to strings of formatives rather than strings of phones." *Formative* is defined in the first paragraph of the book as a "minimal syntactically functioning unit." The problem of one word or other short sentences is likewise slid over. Here is what he says about kernal sentences:

> These are sentences of a particularly simple sort that involve a minimum of transformational apparatus in their generation. The notion "kernal sentence" has, I think, an important intuitive significance, but since kernal sentences play no distinctive role in generation or interpretation of sentences, I shall say nothing about them here.[7]

Chomsky gives us no idea as to what the important intuitive significance of kernal sentences might be.

Milka Ivić's figure of 160 active definitions of the sentence arises from the work of John Ries, who first published *Was Ist Ein Satz?* in 1894, more than a decade before Saussure, and who updated it in Prague in 1931. Ries analyzed 140 definitions in the latter edition, and the 20 further definitions Ivić located were critiques of Ries' analysis. Simeon Potter follows this debate in *Modern Linguistics*, which has an entire chapter devoted to sentence structure.

> The sentence is the chief unit of speech. It may be defined simply as a *minimum complete utterance*. . . . When we assert that the sentence is a minimum complete utterance, or a segment of speech-flow between pause and pause, or an inherited structure into which word-forms are fitted, we are not saying all that might be said about it. Nevertheless, these definitions are probably more workable than John Ries' final effort: "A sentence is a grammatically constructed minimum speech-unit which expresses its content in respect to that content's relation to reality." We may, in fact, find as much difficulty in defining a sentence as in pin-pointing a phoneme, and yet, after a little training, we all recognize phonemes and sentences when we see them.[8]

In short, the history and structure of linguistics as a profession inhibits, if it doesn't entirely prevent, an elaboration of a theory of the sentence which might then be applied to literature.

As early as the late 1920's, the Russian linguist Valentin Vološinov proposed this critique in *Marxism and the Philosophy of Language*:

> Traditional principles and methods in linguistics do not provide grounds for a productive approach to the problems of syntax. This is particularly true of Abstract Objectivism [his term for the Saussurian school], where the traditional methods and principles have found their most distinct and consistent expression. All the fundamental categories of modern linguistic thought . . . are thoroughly phonetic and morphological. . . . In consequence, the study of syntax is in a very bad state . . . .
>   In point of fact, of all the forms of language, the syntactic forms are the ones closest to the concrete form of utterence . . . productive

study of syntactic forms is only possible on the grounds of a fully elaborated theory of utterance . . . .

Linguistic thinking has hoplessly lost any sense of the verbal whole.[9]

Vološinov by-passes the sentence more or less entirely, writing that "the category of sentence is merely a definition of the sentence as a unit-element *within* an utterance, and not by any means as a whole entity."

The function of the sentence as a *unit within a larger structure* will, in fact, become important when we look at the role of the *new* sentence. But what is vital here is the failure, even within this critical analysis, for a possible theory of the sentence.

At this point, a number of things can be stated with regard to the sentence and linguistics:

1) The sentence is a term derived from writing, which in linguistics is often brought over to the study of speech. Specifically, the sentence is a unit of writing.

2) There exists in speech an open-ended form like, but not identical with, the sentence of writing. Following Vološinov, I am going to refer to it as the utterance.

The critical difference between the utterance and the sentence is that the utterance is indeterminate, a chain that can be more or less indefinitely extended. There is no sentence but a determinate sentence and this is fixed by the period.

3) The focus in linguistics on the development of a description of *langue* over *parole,* and the non-addressing of the question of writing has rendered the question of the sentence invisible.

If linguistics fails to deal with the sentence because it fails to separate writing from speech, philosophy deals with language neither as speech nor writing. Language is either:

1) Thought itself
  a) sometimes understood as constricted and formal, as in logic or a calculus, e.g., Quine's "austure canonical scheme," by which, if one only knew the complete set of proper eternal sentences, one could logically construct the whole of possible correct knowledge;

b) sometimes understood as unconstricted, as when language is taken to be identical with the sum of possible thought, a position Chomsky takes in his forays into philosophic discourse.

2) A manifestation or transformation of thought, also breaking down into a constricted or unconstricted models, Wittgenstein being an example of both, constricted in his early *Tractatus* and unconstricted in *Philosophical Investigations* both of which argue that language is a disguise for thought.

Wittgenstein's model, in both his early and late writings, closely parallels that of Saussure. The dramatic shift between these periods is one of object and goal—from the disentangling of an idealized discourse in the *Tractatus* to an exploration of the problems of meaning in the actual use of language in *Philosophical Investigations*. The break comes in the '30s and is documented in *Philosophical Grammar* and its appendices. The following sections from the *Investigations* show how close some of his later work comes toward a type of discussion that surrounds the new sentence:

498. When I say that the orders "Bring me sugar" and "Bring me milk" make sense, but not the combination "Milk me sugar," that does not mean that the utterance of this combination has no effect. And if its effect is that the other person stares at me and gapes, I don't on that account call it the order to stare and gape, even if that was precisely the effect I wanted to produce.
499. To say "This combination of words makes no sense" excludes it from the sphere of language and thereby bounds the domain of language. But when one draws a boundary it may be for various kinds of reasons. If I surround an area with a fence or a line or otherwise, the purpose may be to prevent someone from getting in or out; but it may also be part of a game and the players be supposed, say, to jump over the boundary; or it may shew where the property of one man ends and that of another begins and so on. So if I draw a boundary line that is not yet to say what it is for.[10]

One of the things that makes Wittgenstein (and, more recently, Jacques Derrida) so useful, suggestive and quotable to poets is the high degree of metaphor in his work. Not all philosophical discourse is like that—in fact, most shuns it.

A.J. Ayer wrote in this latter style. In *Language, Truth and Logic*, he tried to separate sentences from propositions from statements, a classic attempt at the compartmentalization of connotation:

> Thus I propose that any form of words that is grammatically significant shall be held to constitute a sentence, and that every indicative sentence, whether it is literally meaningful or not, shall be regarded as expressing a statement. Furthermore, any two sentences which are mutually translatable will be said to express the same statement. The word "proposition," on the other hand, will be reserved for what is expressed by sentences which are literally meaningful.[11]

This formula for the sentence is no more well-defined than any from linguistics. It does not even propose the possibility of a distinction between a simple sentence, a compound or a fragment, since it doesn't address the question of a full-pause or maximum grammatical integration of meaning. But it does draw a sharp line between the categories proposed, or at least attempts to. Yet even this succinct formulation has resisted acceptance:

> Ayer says (a) that his use "proposition" designates a class of sentences that all have *the same meaning* and (b) that "consequently" he speaks of propositions, not sentences, as being true or false. But of course what a sentence *means* does *not* enable us to say that *it is* true or false. . . . [12]

The problems posed by making sentences synonymous, or even approximate, with propositions can be viewed in an extreme form in Willard Van Orman Quine's *Word and Object*:

> A sentence is not an event of utterance, but a universal. . . . In general, to specify a proposition without dependence on circumstances of utterance, we put . . . an *eternal* sentence: a sentence whose truth value stays fixed through time and from speaker to speaker.[13]

Literary criticism ought to serve as a corrective. Unlike philosophy, it is a discourse with a clearly understood material object. Like philosophy, it is centuries old as a discipline. In addition, it is fortuitously situated in western societies, where literature is treated in the schools as an extension of language learning.

71

As Jonathan Culler cautions in *Structuralist Poetics*, literary criticism is the study of reading, not writing. If a theory of the sentence is to be found in poetics, it won't necessarily be of great use to writers. However, it might function as the basis on which to create such a theory.

I want to consider first the New Critics, partly because they were so dominant that, until recently, all other critical tendencies were defined by the nature of their opposition. The New Critics were strongly influenced by the British philosophical tradition, with I.A. Richards, for example, playing a major role in both communities. In addition, René Wellek was a product of the Prague school of linguistics, and as such was thoroughly familiar with the work of Saussure on the one hand, and Shklovsky on the other, both of whom are cited with approval in Wellek's *Theory of Literature*, written with Austin Warren.

These influences already suggest that the *Theory of Literature* is not going to contain a coherent theory of the sentence. The Saussurian model of linguistics is implicit in this famous dictum:

Every work of art is, first of all, a series of *sounds* out of which arises the meaning.[14]

This does not, as it might have, lead them toward an examination of syntax—let alone sentences. But it does put them in the unenviable position of defending a point of view from which their own assertion could easily have been attacked.

Wellek and Warren are aware of this reduction, and defend themselves with a little sleight of hand, arguing that:

A . . . common assumption, that sound should be analysed in complete divorce from meaning, is also false.[15]

This does not, as it might have, lead them toward an examination of syntax—let alone sentences. But it does put them in the unenviable position of defending a point of view from which their own assertion could easily have been attacked.

Theory of Literature is not a theory of writing. In part, this is due to the accurate perception that not all literature is written. Nonetheless, Wellek and Warren fail to address the specific changes which occur once literature is submitted to the writing process. They justify this by arguing that the written text is never the "real" work. This also enables them to put aside any consideration of the impact of printing on literature, beyond the most off-hand acknowledgment of its existence. Viktor Shklovsky notes the importance of this exclusion in an interview in the Winter 1978-79 issue of *The Soviet Review*:

> At one time only poetry was recognized, and prose was regarded as something second class, for it seemed a counterfeit; for a long time it was not admitted into high art. It was let in only when they started printing books. [16]

If we argue—and I am arguing—that the sentence, as distinct from the utterance of speech, is a unit of prose, and if prose as literature and the rise of printing are inextricably interwoven, then the impact of printing on literature, not just on the presentation of literature, but on how writing itself is written, needs to be addressed. This would be the historical component of any theory of the sentence.

Wellek and Warren avoid any such discussion. Instead, they divide literature into a binary scheme, one side devoted to character and plot construction, the other devoted to wordplay. Generally speaking, these become the axes of fiction and poetry. This parallels Saussure's division of language into a paradigmatic and a syntagmatic axis. And it also parallels the strategies of Structuralism.

Wordplay, the paradigmatic axis of poetry, could itself lead toward an investigation of the sentence, but it doesn't. The realms Wellek and Warren carry it to are image, metaphor, symbol and myth: successively broader groups of referentiality.

Like New Criticism, Structuralism—and here I mean structuralist poetics—is founded on the model of linguistics first constructed by Saussure and later codified by Louis Hjemslev and Roman Jakobson. However, it has several practical advantages over New Criticism: it is not heavily influenced by the British school of philosophy; it has not identified itself with the conservative movement in literature; and it is at least conscious of the critique of Saussurian linguistics posed by Derrida.

Structuralism has come closer to a recognition of the need for a theory of the sentence than any of the tendencies thus far examined. But this doesn't mean one has been developed. Following a division made by Wellek and Warren of discourse into three broad categories—everyday, scientific, and literary—Pierre Machery in *Theory of Literary Production* proposes that everyday discourse is ideological, scientific discourse is empirical, and literary discourse moves back and forth between these two poles. This model echoes the one made by Louis Zukofsky of his work having a lower limit of speech and an upper one of music. Machery's revision makes a real distinction and moves it well towards something that could be put into a contextualized theory of utterance such as that proposed by Vološinov. But Machery's divisions are inaccurate.

Everyday discourse is purely ideological, but so too is all specialized discourse. The constraints posed on all modes of professional jargon and technical language, whether scientific, legal, medical or whatever, communicate class *in addition to* any other object of their discourse. There is no such thing as a non-ideological or value-free discourse.

Tzvestan Todorov's *The Poetics of Prose* actually addresses the function of the sentence, for about two paragraphs. Todorov defines meaning according to the formula of Emile Beneviste: "It is the capacity of a linguistic unit to integrate a higher-level unit." In a 1966 lecture at John Hopkins, Todorov demonstrates his understanding of the importance of the question of integration:

> While in speech the integration of units does not go beyond the sentence, in literature sentences are integrated again as part of larger articulations, and the latter in their turn into units of greater dimension, and so on until we have the entire work . . . On the other hand, the interpretations of each unit are innumerable, for their comprehension depends on the system in which it will be included.[17]

Consider, for example, how meaning is altered when the same words are integrated into successively longer strings:

Someone called Douglas.
Someone called Douglas over.
He was killed by someone called Douglas over in Oakland.

Of Structuralist critics, the late Roland Barthes was the most explicit in calling for a theory of the sentence. In the same symposium with Todorov, he went so far as to say:

> The structure of the sentence, the object of linguistics, is found again, homologically, in the structure of works. Discourse is not simply an adding together of sentences; it is, itself, one great sentence.[18]

This statement has the glaring flaw that the sentence has not been the object of linguistics, and Barthes was deliberately being audacious in his statement. But here is an important insight, which is that the modes of integration which carry words into phrases and phrases into sentences are not fundamentally different from those by which an individual sentence integrates itself into a larger work. This not only gives us a good reason for demanding a theory of sentences, but also suggests that such a theory would lead us toward a new mode of analysis of literary products themselves.

In *S/Z,* Barthes demonstrates how a structuralist interpretation of a specific story ought to proceed. He takes Balzac's "Sarrasine" and analyzes it according to several different codes. In a sense, he goes word by word through the text, but he does *not* break his analysis into sentences. Instead, he uses what he calls *lexias,* anywhere from one word to several sentences long. Barthes himself describes the selection as being "arbitrary in the extreme," although he treats them as "units of reading."

His earliest work, *Writing Degree Zero*, does address the question of the sentence, but in a highly metaphoric style and with a certain primitiveness, really only a reflection of the other work which had been done in this area in the past 25 years. Compare this passage with Beneviste's theory of integration:

> The economy of classical language . . . is relational, which means that in it words are abstracted as much as possible in the interest of relationships. In it, no word has a density by itself, it is hardly the sign of a thing, but rather the means of conveying a connection. Far from plunging into an inner reality consubstantial to its outer configuration, it extends, as soon as it is uttered, towards other words. . . .
>
> Modern poetry, since it must be distinguished from classical poetry and from any type of prose, destroys the spontaneously functional nature of language, and leaves standing only its lexical basis. It retains only the outward shape of relationships, their music, but not their reality. The Word shines forth above a line of relationships emptied of their content, grammar is bereft of its purpose, it becomes prosody and is no longer anything but an

inflexion which lasts only to present the Word.[19]

Barthes is here casting against the temporal plane of history a proposition originally formulated by Roman Jakobson for all poetry, that "the poetic function projects the principle of equivalence from the axis of selection into the axis of combination." Jakobson's dictum suggests the primacy of the *paradigmatic* to the extent that it imposes itself on the supposed value-free combinations of the *syntagmatic*.

Barthes suggests that Jakobson's projection of the paradigm is not a constant, but that history has seen the movement from a syntagmatic focus to a paradigmatic one, and that a break has occurred at a point when some critical mass—not specifically identified by Barthes—rendered it impossible for units to continue to integrate beyond grammatical levels, e.g., the sentence. It is just this breach—when the signifier, freed suddenly from its servitude to an integrating hierarchy of syntactic relations, finds itself drained of any signified—that Frederic Jameson identifies as the characteristic feature of postmodernism:

> The crisis in historicity now dictates a return . . . to the question of temporal organization in general in the postmodern force field, and indeed, to the problem of the form that time, temporality and the syntagmatic will be able to take in a culture increasingly dominated by space and spatial logic. If, indeed, the subject has lost its capacity actively to extend its pro-tensions and re-tensions across the temporal manifold, and to organize its past and future into coherent experience, it becomes difficult enough to see how the cultural productions of such a subject could result in anything but 'heaps of fragments' and in a practice of the randomly heterogeneous and fragmentary and the aleatory. These are, however, very precisely some of the privileged terms in which postmodernist cultural production has been analysed (and even defended, by its own apologists).[20]

How do sentences integrate into higher units of meaning? The obvious first step here is toward the paragraph:

> . . . in certain crucial respects paragraphs are analogues to exchanges in dialogue. The paragraph is something like a vitiated dialogue worked into the body of a monologic utterance. Behind the device of

partitioning speech into units, which are termed paragraphs in their written form, lie orientation toward listener or reader and calculation of the latter's possible reactions.[21]

Vološinov's definition is not radically different from partitioning strategies in some current work, such as David Bromige's essay poems. David Antin, in his talk at 80 Langton Street, described his own work in just Vološinov's terms, as a vitiated dialogue.

Ferrucio Rossi-Landi, the Italian semiotician, focuses on this problem more closely when he argues that the *syllogism* is the classic paradigm for above-sentence integration. For example, the sentences "All women were once girls" and "Some women are lawyers" logically lead to a third sentence or conclusion, a higher level of meaning: "Some lawyers were once girls." Literature proceeds by suppression, most often, of this third term, positing instead chains of the order of the first two. Here is a paragraph by Barrett Watten:

He thought they were a family unit. There were seven men and four women, and thirteen children in the house. Which voice was he going to record?[22]

The first sentence provides a subject, "He," plus a complex object, "they," who may or may not be "a family unit." The second depicts a plurality ("they"), which might or might not be "a family unit." The third again presents a subject identified as "he" in the context of a question ("Which voice") which implies a plurality. Yet any integration of these sentences into a tidy little narrative is, in fact, a presumption on the part of the reader. Neither of the last two sentences has any clear term of anaphor, pointing back inescapably to a previous sentence. In the next paragraph, Watten explores the reader's recognition of this presumptiveness, this willingness to "complete the syllogism":

That's why we talk language. Back in Sofala I'm writing this down wallowing in a soft leather armchair. A dead dog lies in the gutter, his feet in the air.[23]

Here the first sentence proposes itself, by virtue of its grammar, as a conclusion, although it is by no means self-evident why this is "why we talk language." The second starts with a phrase, "Back in Sofala," indicating a shift on the part of the subject in both time and place. But now the subject is "I." The third sentence, which shares with the previous two only its use of the present tense, is a comic editorial on the process itself: referentiality is not merely dead, it makes for a silly corpse. Yet just two paragraphs above, the logical distance between sentences had been so great as to suppress all but the most ambitious attempts at readerly integration:

> The burden of classes is the twentieth-century career. He can be incredibly cruel. Events are advancing at a terrifying rate.[24]

Rossi-Landi offers us another approach to the sentence. *Linguistics and Economics* argues that language-use arises from the need to divide labor in the community, and that the elaboration of language-systems and of labor production, up to and including all social production, follow parallel paths. In this view, the completed tool is a sentence.

A hammer, for example, consists of a face, a handle, and a peen. Without the presence of all three, the hammer will not function. Sentences relate to their subunits in just this way. Only the manufacturer of hammers would have any use for disconnected handles; thus without the whole there can be no exchange value. Likewise, it is at the level of the sentence that the use value and the exchange value of any statement unfold into view. The child's one-word sentence is communicative precisely because (and to the degree that) it represents a whole. Any further subdivision would leave one with an unuseable and incomprehensible fragment.

Yet longer sentences are themselves composed of words, many, if not all, of which, *in other contexts*, might form adequate one-word sentences. Thus the sentence is the hinge unit of any literary product.

Larger productions, such as poems, are like completed machines. Any individual sentence might be a piston. It will not get you down the road by itself, but you could not move the vehicle without it.

The sentence is a unit of writing. Yet the utterance exists as a unit of speech prior to the acquisition of writing, for both individuals and societies. The utterances of *Gilgamesh* or the Homeric epics would appear to have been translated without great difficulty into written sentence form long before the advent of creative or aesthetic prose. Nonetheless, it is the hypotactic logic of the prose sentence, prose paragraph and expository essay which is most completely the model through which the sentence is communicated in western societies by means of the organized process of education. "Correct grammar," which has never existed in spoken daily life save as a template, is itself thus predicated upon a model of "high" discourse. (As Shklovsky noted, prose entered the literary arena with the rise of printing only a little more than 500 years ago; its cultural role became progressively more important as literacy spread to the lower classes.) "Educated" speech imitates writing: the more "refined" the individual, the more likely their utterances will possess the characteristics of expository prose. The sentence, hypotactic and complete, was and still is an index of class in society. Accordingly, the function of this unit within creative prose proves essential to our understanding of how a sentence might become "new."

Prose fiction to a significant extent derives from the narrative epics of poetry, but moves toward a very different sense of form and organization. Exterior formal devices, such as rhyme and linebreak, diminish, and the structural units become the sentence and paragraph. In the place of external devices, which function to keep the reader's or listener's experience at least partly in the present, consuming the text, most fiction foregrounds the syllogistic leap, or integration above the level of the sentence, to create a fully referential tale.

This does not mean that the fictive paragraph is without signficant form, even in the most compelling narrative. Consider this paragraph from Conrad's *The Secret Agent*:

In front of the great doorway a dismal row of newspaper sellers standing clear of the pavement dealt out their wares from the gutter. It was a raw, gloomy day of the early spring; and the grimy sky, the mud of the streets, the rags of the dirty men harmonized excellently with the eruption of the damp, rubbishy sheets of paper soiled with printers' ink. The posters, maculated with filth, garnished like tapestry the sweep of the curbstone. The trade in afternoon papers was brisk, yet, in comparison with the swift, constant march of foot traffic, the effect was of indifference, of disregarded distribution. Ossipon looked hurriedly both ways before stepping out into the cross-currents, but the Professor was already out of sight.[25]

Only the last of these five sentences actually furthers the narrative. The rest serve to set the scene, but do so in the most formal manner imaginable. Every sentence is constructed around some kind of opposition. The first takes us from the "great doorway" to a "dismal row" in the "gutter." The second contrasts "spring" with "raw and gloomy," and then has the "grimy sky," "the mud," "the rags of the dirty men" "harmonize excellently" with the "damp rubbishy sheets soiled with ink." And so forth, even to the presence of Ossipon and the absence of the Professor.

This kind of structure might well be foregrounded in a poem, by placing key terms in critical places along the line, by putting certain oppositions in literal rhyme, and by writing the whole perhaps in the present tense. Fiction has a much greater tendency toward the past tense in general. More importantly, the lack of these foregrounding devices permits the syllogistic capacity of the language to become dominant.

It is this condition of prose that we find also in the work of Russell Edson, the best known English language writer of the prose poem. This is from "The Sardine Can Dormitory":

> A man opens a sardine can and finds a row of tiny cots full of tiny dead people; it is a dormitory flooded with oil.
>
> He lifts out the tiny bodies with a fork and lays them on a slice of bread; puts a leaf of lettuce over them, and closes the sandwich with another slice of bread.
>
> He wonders what he should do with the tiny cots; wondering if they are not eatable, too?
>
> He looks into the can and sees a tiny cat floating in the oil. The bottom of the can, under the oil, is full of little shoes and stockings.[26]

Other than the hallucinated quality of the tale, derived from surrealism and the short stories of Kafka, there is really nothing here of great difference from the conditions of prose as one finds it in fiction. If anything, it uses fewer formal devices than the Conrad passage above.

In good part, what makes Edson a prose poet is where he publishes. The poems in *Edson's Mentality* were first published in *Poetry Now*, *Oink!*, and *The Iowa Review*. By publishing among poets, Edson has taken on the public role of a poet, but a poet whose work participates entirely in the tactics and units of fiction.

Edson is a good example of why the prose poem—even that name is awkward—has come to be thought of as a bastard form.

Even today in America the prose poem barely has any legitimacy. There are no prose poems at all in Hayden Carruth's anthology, *The Voice That Is Great Within Us*.

Nor in Donald Allen's *The New American Poetry*.

Nor in the Robert Kelly/Paris Leary anthology, *A Controversy of Poets*.

The prose poem came into existence in France. From 1699, the rules of versification set down by the French Academy proved so rigid that some writers simply chose to sidestep them, composing instead in a "poetic" prose style, writing epics and pastorals in this mode in the 18th Century. At the same time, poetry from other languages was being translated into French prose. It was Aloysius Bertrand who, in 1827, first began to compose poems in prose. He published these works in a book called *Gaspard de la Nuit*. By the end of the 19th Century, the genre had been incorporated fully into French literature by Baudelaire, Mallarmé, and Rimbaud.

The French found the prose poem to be an ideal device for the dematerialization of writing. Gone were the external devices of form that naggingly held the reader in the present, aware of the physical presence of the text itself. Sentences could be lengthened, stretched even further than the already extensive elocutions which characterized Mallarmé's verse, without befuddling the reader or disengaging her from the poem. And longer sentences also suspended for greater periods of time the pulse of closure which enters into prose as the mark of rhythm. It was perfect for hallucinated, fantastic and dreamlike contents, for pieces with multiple locales and times squeezed into a few words. Here is a six sentence poem by Mallarmé, translated by Keith Bosley as "The Pipe":

Yesterday I found my pipe as I was dreaming about a long evening's work, fine winter work. Throwing away cigarettes with all the childish joys of summer into the past lit by sun-blue leaves, the muslin dresses and taking up again my earnest pipe as a serious man who wants a long undisturbed smoke, in order to work better: but I was not expecting the surprise this abandoned creature was preparing, hardly had I taken the first puff when I forgot my great books to be done, amazed, affected, I breathed last winter coming back. I had not touched the faithful friend since my return to France, and all London, London as I lived the whole of it by myself, a year ago appeared; first the dear fogs which snugly wrap our brains and have there, a smell of their own, when they get in under the casement. My tobacco smelt of a dark room with leather furniture seasoned by coaldust on which the lean black cat luxuriated; the big fires! and the maid with red arms tipping out the coals, and the noise of these coals falling from the steel scuttle into the iron grate in the morning—the time of the postman's solemn double knock, which brought me to life! I saw again through the windows those sick trees in the deserted square—I saw the open sea, so often crossed that winter, shivering on the bridge of the steamer wet with drizzle and blackened by smoke—with my poor wandering loved one, in travelling clothes with a long dull dress the color of road dust, a cloak sticking damp to her cold shoulders, one of those straw hats without a feather and almost without ribbons, which rich ladies throw away on arrival, so tattered are they by the sea air and which poor loved ones retrim for a few good seasons more. Round her neck was wound the terrible handkerchief we wave when we say goodbye for ever.[27]

Here we almost have a prefiguring of the new sentence: the absence of external poetic devices, but not their interiorization in the sentence as in Conrad. Mallarmé has extended their absence by reducing the text to the minimum number of sentences. The de-emphasis on the materiality of the text in this manner is an example of prose shaping poetic form and beginning to alter sentence structure. But note that there is no attempt whatsoever to prevent the integration of linguistic units into higher levels. These sentences take us not toward the recognition of language, but away from it.

The prose poem did not soon take root in England or America. Nonetheless, Oscar Wilde and Amy Lowell made stabs at it, and the presence of poems from other languages being translated into English *prose*, such as Tagore's rendering of Indian songs, *Gitanjali*, was quite visible.

Alfred Kreymbourg's 1930 anthology, *Lyric America*, has four prose poems. One is a long and tedious one by Arturo Giovanni, called "The Walker." The other three are by the black poet Fenton Johnson. Johnson uses a device which points in the direction of the new sentence. Each sentence is a complete paragraph; run-on sentences are treated as one paragraph each, but two paragraphs begin with conjunctions. Structured thus, Johnson's is the first

American prose poem with a clear, if simple, sentence:paragraph relation.

THE MINISTER

I mastered pastoral theology, the Greek of the Apostles, and all the difficult subjects in a minister's curriculum.

I was learned as any in this country when the Bishop ordained me.

And I went to preside over Mount Moriah, largest flock in the Conference.

I preached the Word as I felt it, I visited the sick and dying and comforted the afflicted in spirit.

I loved my work because I loved God.

But I lost my charge to Sam Jenkins, who has not been to school four years in his life.

I lost my charge because I could not make my congregation shout.

And my dollar money was small, very small.

Sam Jenkins can tear a Bible to tatters and his congregation destroys the pews with their shouting and stamping.

Sam Jenkins leads in the gift of raising dollar money.

Such is religion.[28]

Johnson is clearly influenced by Edgar Lee Masters, but his sentence:paragraph device brings the reader's attention back time and again to the voice of the narrator in this poem. It is the first instance in English of a prose poem which calls attention to a discursive or poetic effect. Even though the referential content is always evident, the use of the paragraph here limits the reader's ability to get away from the language itself.

Yet Fenton Johnson may not be the first American prose poet of consequence. Here, from *Kora in Hell: Improvisations* is the third entry in the twentieth grouping, accompanied by its commentary:

One need not be hopelessly cast down because he cannot cut onyx into a ring to fit a lady's finger. You hang your head. There is neither onyx nor porphyry on these roads—only brown dirt. For all that, one may see his face in a flower along it—even in this light. Eyes only and for a flash only. Oh, keep the neck bent, plod with the back to the split dark! Walk in the curled mudcrusts to one side, hand hanging.

Ah well . . . Thoughts are trees! Ha, ha, ha, ha! Leaves load the branches and upon them white night sits kicking her heels against the shore.

A poem can be made of anything. This is a portrait of a disreputable farm hand made out of the stuff of his environment.[29]

Certainly we have strategies here which echo the French prose poem, such as the constantly shifting point of view. More important: the sentences allow only the most minimal syllogistic shift to the level of reference, and some, such as the laughter, permit no such shift whatsoever.

But note the word "portrait" in Williams' commentary. His model here is not the French prose poem so much as the so-called cubist prose of Gertrude Stein, who as early as 1911 wrote *Tender Buttons*:

CUSTARD

Custard is this. It has aches, aches when. Not to be. Not to be narrowly. This makes a whole little hill.

It is better than a little thing that has mellow real mellow. It is better than lakes whole lakes, it is better than seeding.

ROAST POTATOES

Roast potatoes for.[30]

Stein says in "Poetry and Grammar" that she did not intend to make *Tender Buttons* poetry, but it just happened that way. It is sufficiently unlike much that she later called poetry to suggest that it is something other than that. The portraits *are* portraits. The syllogistic move above the sentence level to an exterior reference is possible, but the nature of the book reverses the direction of this movement. Rather than making the shift in an automatic and gestalt sort of way, the reader is forced to deduce it from the partial views and associations posited in each sentence. The portrait of custard is marvelously accurate.

The sentences deserve some examination. They are fragmented in a way that is without precedent in English. Who but Stein would have written a sentence in 1911 that ends in the middle of a prepositional phrase? Her use of elliptical sentences—"Not to be. Not to be narrowly."—deliberately leaves the subject out of sight. Custard does not want to be a hard fact. And the anaphoric pronoun of "this makes a whole little hill" refers not to custard, but the negated verb phrases of the two previous sentences. Likewise in "Roast Potatoes," Stein uses the preposition "for" to convert "roast" from an adjective into a verb.

Stein has written at great length about sentences and paragraphs. Her essays on them are works in themselves, and in them, she reveals herself to have thought more seriously about the differences here than any other poet in English.

Because of the consciously non-expository method of her arguments, I'm going to simply quote, in order, some passages which shed light on the issue in the terms through which we have been approaching it. From "Sentences and Paragraphs," a section of *How To Write* (1931):

1) Within itself. A part of a sentence may be sentence without their meaning.
2) Every sentence has a beginning. Will he begin.
   Every sentence which has a beginning makes it be left more to them.
3) A sentence should be arbitrary it should not please be better.
4) The difference between a short story and a paragraph. There is none.
5) There are three kinds of sentences are there. Do sentences follow the three. There are three kinds of sentences. Are there three kinds of sentences that follow the three.[31]

This of course refers to the simple, compound, complex division of traditional grammars.

From the essay "Sentences" in the same book:

6) A sentence is an interval in which there is finally forward and back. A sentence is an interval during which if there is a difficulty they will do away with it. A sentence is a part of the way when they wish to be secure. A sentence is their politeness in asking for a cessation. And when it happens they look up.
7) There are two kinds of sentences. When they go. They are given to me. There are these two kinds of sentences. Whenever they go

they are given to me. There are there these two kinds of sentences there. One kind is when they like and the other kind is as often as they please. The two kinds of sentences relate when they manage to be for less with once whenever they are retaken. Two kinds of sentences make it do neither of them dividing in a noun.[32]

Stein is here equating clauses, which divide as indicated into dependent and independent, with sentences. Anything as high up the chain of language as a clause is already partially a kind of sentence. It can move syllogistically as a sentence in itself to a higher order of meaning. That's an important and original perception.

8) Remember a sentence should not have a name. A name is familiar. A sentence should not be familiar. All names are familiar there for there should not be a name in a sentence. If there is a name in a sentence a name which is familiar makes a data and therefor there is no equilibrium.[33]

This explains Stein's distaste for nouns quite adequately. The concern for equilibrium is an example of grammar as meter, which points us clearly toward the new sentence.

In her 1934 American lecture, "Poetry and Grammar," Stein makes a few additional comments which cast light on the relation of sentences to prose, and hence prose poems. The first is, I believe, the best single statement on the problem as it is faced by a writer:

9) What had periods to do with it. Inevitably no matter how completely I had to have writing go on, physically one had to again and again stop sometime and if one had to again and again stop some time then periods had to exist. Besides I had always liked the look of periods and I liked what they did. Stopping sometime did not really keep one from going on, it was nothing that interfered, it was only something that happened, and as it happened as a perfectly natural happening, I did believe in periods and I used them. I never really stopped using them.
10) Sentences and paragraphs. Sentences are not emotional but paragraphs are. I can say that as often as I like and it always remains as it is, something that is.

I said I found this out in listening to Basket my dog drinking. And anybody listening to any dog's drinking will see what I mean.[34]

86

Stein later gives some examples of sentences she has written, also from *How To Write* which exist as one sentence paragraphs and capture the balance between the unemotional sentence and the emotional paragraph. My favorite is "A dog which you have never had before has sighed."

> 11) We do know a little now what prose is. Prose is the balance the emotional balance that makes the reality of paragraphs and the unemotional balance that makes the reality of sentences and having realized completely realized that sentences are not emotional while paragraphs are, prose can be the essential balance that is made inside something that combines the sentence and the paragraph . . . . [35]

What Stein means about paragraphs being emotional and sentences not is precisely the point made by Emile Beneviste: that linguistic units integrate only up to the level of the sentence, but higher orders of meaning—such as emotion—integrate at higher levels than the sentence and occur only in the presence of either many sentences or, at least Stein's example suggests this, in the presence of certain complex sentences in which dependent clauses integrate with independent ones.*The sentence is the horizon*, the border between these two fundamentally distinct types of integration.

So what is the *new* sentence? It has to do with prose poetry, but not necessarily prose poems, at least not in the restricted and narrow sense of that category. It does not have to do with the prose poems of the Surrealists, which manipulate meaning only at the "higher" or "outer" layers, well beyond the horizon of the sentence. Nor with the non-surrealist prose poems of the Middle-American variety, such as the dramatic monologs of James Wright or David Ignatow, which do likewise.

Bob Grenier's *Sentences* directly anticipates the new sentence. By removal of context, Grenier prevents most leaps beyond the level of grammatic integration. This is the extreme case for the new sentence. However, most of Grenier's "sentences" are more properly utterances, and in that sense follow Olson, Pound and a significant portion of Creeley's work. Periodically, some sentences and paragraphs in Creeley's *A Day Book* and *Presences* carry the pressurized quality of the new sentence, in that the convolutions of syntax often suggest the internal presence of once-exteriorized poetic forms, although here identified much with the features of speech.

Another author whose works anticipate this mode is Hannah Weiner, particularly in her diaristic prose pieces where the flow of sentences (their syntactic completion, let alone integration into larger units) is radically disrupted by "alien" discourses which she ascribes to "clairvoyance." While, in general, the new sentence has not been nearly as visible on the East Coast as it has in the west, something much like or tending towards it can be found in the writings of several poets, including Peter Seaton, Bruce Andrews, Diane Ward, Bernadette Mayer (especially in her early books), James Sherry, Lynne Dreyer, Alan Davies, Charles Bernstein and Clark Coolidge.

A paragraph from section XVIII of Coolidge's "Weathers":

> At most a book the porch. Flames that are at all rails of snow. Flower down winter to vanish. Mite hand stroking flint to a card. Names that it blue. Wheel locked to pyramid through stocking the metal realms. Hit leaves. Participle.[36]

In other contexts, any of these could become a new sentence, in the sense that any sentence properly posed and staged could. Each focuses attention at the level of the language in front of the reader. But seldom at the level of the sentence. Mostly at the levels of phrase and clause. "Flower down winter to vanish" can be a grammatical sentence in the traditional sense if flower is taken as a verb and the sentence as a command. But "Names that it blue" resists even that much integrating energy. Coolidge refuses to carve connotative domains from words. They are still largely decon-textualized—save for the physical-acoustic elements—readymades.

This is not an example of the new sentence because it works primarily below the level of the sentence. However, there is another important element here as a result: the length of sentences and the use of the period are now wholly rhythmic. Grammar has become, to recall Barthes' words, prosody. As we shall see, this is an element whenever the new sentence is present.

Here, from Bob Perelman's *a.k.a.*, are two paragraphs of new sentences:

> An inspected geography leans in with the landscapes's repetitions. He lived here, under the assumptions. The hill suddenly vanished, proving him right. I was left holding the bag. I peered into it.
>
> The ground was approaching fast. It was a side of himself he

rarely showed. The car's tracks disappeared in the middle of the road. The dialog with objects is becoming more strained. Both sides gather their forces. Clouds enlarge. The wind picks up. He held onto the side of the barn by his fingertips.[37]

Here we note these qualities: (1) The paragraph organizes the sentences in fundamentally the same way a stanza does lines of verse. There are roughly the same number of sentences in each paragraph and the number is low enough to establish a clear sentence:paragraph ratio. Why is this not simply a matter of the way sentences are normally organized into paragraphs? Because there is no specific referential focus. The paragraph here is a unit of measure—as it was also in "Weathers." (2) The sentences are all sentences: the syntax of each resolves *up* *to* the level of the sentence. Not that these sentences "make sense" in the ordinary way. For example, "He lived here, under the assumptions." This could be rewritten, or have been derived, from a sentence such as "He lived here, under the elm trees," or, "He lived here, under the assumption *that* etc." (3) This continual torquing of sentences is a traditional quality of poetry, but in poetry it is most often accomplished by linebreaks, or by devices such as rhyme. Here poetic form has moved into the interiors of prose.

Consider, by way of contrast, the first stanza of Alan Bernheimer's "Carapace":

The face of a stranger
is a privilege to see
each breath a signature
and the same sunset fifty years later
though familiarity is an education[38]

There are shifts and torquings here also, but these occur hinged by *external* poetic form: linebreaks. In "Carapace," the individual line is so-called ordinary language and is without this torque or pressurization of syntax. Torquing, the projection of the principle of equivalence from the axis of selection into that of combination, yields, in this instance, sly and carefully-honed incommensurabilities, and occurs in "Carapace" through the *addition* of the lines, one to another.

a.k.a. however, has redeployed the linebreak to two levels. As noted, the length of the sentence is a matter now of quantity, of measure. But the torquing which is normally triggered by linebreaks, the function of which is to enhance ambiguity and polysemy, has moved directly into the grammar of the sentence. At one level, the completed sentence (i.e., not the completed thought, but the maximum level of grammatic/ linguistic integration) has become equivalent to a line, a condition not previously imposed on sentences.

Imagine what the major poems of literary history would look like if each sentence was identical to a line.

That is why an ordinary sentence, such as "I peered into it," can become a new sentence, that is, a sentence with an interior poetic structure in addition to interior ordinary grammatical structure. That is also why and how lines quoted from a Sonoma newspaper in David Bromige's "One Spring" can become new sentences.

In fact, increased sensitivity to syllogistic movement endows works of the new sentence with a much greater capacity to incorporate ordinary sentences of the material world, because here form moves from the whole downward and the disjunction of a quoted sentence from a newspaper puts its referential content (a) into play with its own diction, as in the sentence "Danny always loved Ireland," (b) into play with the preceding and succeeding sentences, as quantity, syntax, and measure; and (c) into play with the paragraph as a whole, now understood as a unit not of logic or argument, but as quantity, a stanza.

Let's look at this play of syllogistic movement:

I was left holding the bag. I peered into it.
The ground was approaching fast. It was a side of himself he rarely showed.

This is not the systematic distortion of the maximum or highest order of meaning, as in surrealism. Rather, each sentence plays with the preceding and following sentence. The first sounds figurative, because of the deliberate use of the cliche. The second, by using both a repetition of the word "I" and the anaphor "it," twists that, making it sound (a) literal and (b) narrative, in that the two sentences appear to refer to an identical content. But the third sentence, which begins the next paragraph, works instead from the direction one might take in looking into a bag and associating from there the sense of gravity one feels looking down, as though falling.

The fourth sentence moves outside the voice of the narrative "I" and presents the sequence of previous sentences as leading to this humorous conclusion. This double-relation of syllogistic movement, which nonetheless does not build up so far as to move the reader away from the level of language itself, is highly typical of the new sentence.

Further, the interior structure of sentences here reflects also how such issues as balance, normally issues of line organization, recast themselves inside sentences. A sentence like "Clouds enlarge" is no less concerned with such balance than those of Grenier's *Sentences*: the word "enlarged" is an ordinary word *en*larged.

Let's list these qualities of the new sentence, then read a poem watching for their presence:

1) The paragraph organizes the sentences;
2) The paragraph is a unity of quantity, not logic or argument;
3) Sentence length is a unit of measure;
4) Sentence structure is altered for torque, or increased polysemy/ ambiguity;
5) Syllogistic movement is: (a) limited; (b) controlled;
6) Primary syllogistic movement is between the preceding and following sentences;
7) Secondary syllogistic movement is toward the paragraph as a whole, or the total work;
8) The limiting of syllogistic movement keeps the reader's attention at or very close to the level of language, that is, most often at the sentence level or below.

My example is the poem "For She," by Carla Harryman. It is one paragraph:

The back of the hand resting on the pillow was not wasted. We couldn't hear each other speak. The puddle in the bathroom, the sassy one. There were many years between us. I stared the stranger into facing up to Maxine, who had come out of the forest wet from bad nights. I came from an odd bed, a vermillion riot attracted to loud dogs. Nonetheless I could pay my rent and provide for him. On this occasion she apologized. An arrangement that did not provoke inspection. Outside on the stagnant water was a motto. He was more than I perhaps though younger. I sweat at amphibians, managed to get home. The sunlight from the window played up his golden curls and a fist screwed over one eye. Right to left and left to right until the sides of her body were circuits. While dazed and hidden in the room, he sang to himself, severe songs, from a history he knew nothing of. Or should I say malicious? Some rustic gravure, soppy but delicate at pause. I wavered, held her up. I tremble, jack him up. Matted wallowings, I couldn't organize the memory. Where does he find his friends? Maxine said to me "but it was just you again." In spite of the cars and the smoke and the many languages, the radio and the appliances, the flat broad buzz of the tracks, the anxiety with which the eyes move to meet the phone and all the arbitrary colors. I am just the same. Unplug the glass, face the docks. I might have been in a more simple schoolyard.[39]

Compare this with the following characterization of the postmodern cultural text by Frederic Jameson:

> The isolated Signifier is no longer an enigmatic state of the world or an incomprehensible yet mesmerizing fragment of language, but rather something closer to a sentence in free-standing isolation.[40]

Yet what endows Harryman's piece with precisely the intensity or power that makes it worthy of our consideration are the many ways in which individual sentences are *not* "in free-standing isolation." The charged use of pronouns, the recurrence of the name Maxine, the utilization of parallel structures ("I wavered, held her up. I tremble, jack him up.") or of terms extending from the same bank of images, notably water, are all methods for enabling *secondary* syllogistic movement to create or convey an overall impression of unity, without which the systematic blocking of the integration of sentences one to another through *primary* syllogistic movement (not how those parallel sentences operate in different tenses, or how the second one turns on that remarkably ambiguous, possibly sexual, verb "jack") would be trivial, without tension, a "heap of fragments." Nonetheless, any attempt to explicate the work as a whole according to some "higher order" of meaning, such as narrative or character, is doomed to sophistry, if not overt incoherence. The new sentence is a decidedly contextual object. Its effects occur as much between, as within, sentences. Thus it reveals that the blank space, between words or sentences, is much more than the 27th letter of the alphabet. It is beginning to explore and articulate just what those hidden capacities might be.

The new sentence first became visible, at least to my eyes, in the poem "Chamber Music" in Barrett Watten's *Decay*. There are, of course, as I have noted, numerous anticipations of this device, such as Watten's use of the line in his early poem, "Factors Influencing the Weather," or in the last books of the late Jack Spicer. More telling, perhaps even a test of its status as a device, has been its evolution, in something less than a decade, throughout an entire poetic community. Unlike, for example, the short enjambed lines of Robert Creeley, which were so widely imitated in the late 60's, the new sentence has successfully resisted any proprietary appropriation. It is in this sense something different, and more, than a style. The new sentence is the first prose technique to identify the signifier (even that of the blank space) as the locus of literary meaning. As such, it reverses the dynamics which have so long been associated with the tyranny of the signified, and is the first method capable of incorporating all the levels of language, both below the horizon of the sentence *and* above:

> Everywhere there are spontaneous literary discussions. Something structurally new is always being referred to. These topics may be my very own dreams, which everyone takes a friendly interest in. The library extends for miles, under the ground.[41]

TOWARDS PROSE

Charles Baudelaire, in his dedication to Arsène Housaye of the 1869 edition of *Paris Spleen*, first broached the idea of the prose poem, born of the miscegenation of those ostensible linguistic opposites, poetry and prose:

> My dear friend, I send you a little work of which no one can say, without doing it an injustice, that it has neither head nor tail, since, on the contrary, everything in it is both head and tail, alternately and reciprocally. I beg you to consider how admirably convenient this combination is for all of us. . . . We can cut wherever we please, I my dreaming, you your manuscript, the reader his reading; for I do not keep the reader's restive mind hanging in suspense on the threads of an interminable and superfluous plot. Take away one vertebra and the two ends of this tortuous fantasy come together again without pain. Chop it into numerous pieces and you will see that each one can get along alone. . . . I take the liberty of dedicating the whole serpent to you. . . .
>
> It was while running through, for the twentieth time at least, the pages of the famous *Gaspard de la Nuit* of Aloysius Bertrand that the idea came to me of attempting something in the same vein. . . .
>
> Which one of us, in his (*sic*) moments of ambition, has not dreamed of the miracle of a poetic prose, musical, without rhythm and without rhyme, supple enough and rugged enough to adapt itself to the lyrical impulses of the soul, the undulations of reverie, the jibes of conscience . . . ?
>
> To tell the truth, however, I am afraid that my envy has not been propitious. From the very beginning I perceived that I was not only far from my mysterious and brilliant model, but was, indeed, doing something (if it can be called *something*) singularly different, an accident which any one else would glory in, no doubt, but which

can only deeply humiliate a mind convinced that the greatest honor
for a poet is to succeed in doing exactly what he set out to do.[1]

Providing the reader with origin and orientation, Baudelaire
delivers us the prose poem, encased, even at its moment of birth, in
the trappings of history and limits of theory, confinements which
still serve 116 years later to filter and distort perceptions of the
growing body of work which accumulates in its name.

Confusion is the norm, at least in America, when it comes to
determining both what gets to be counted as a prose poem, and
what gets to be considered a poem when and if it should happen to
appear in a prose format. Michael Benedikt's anthology, *The Prose
Poem*,[2] for example, the only booklength collection generally
available in English, omits any work from Gertrude Stein's *Tender
Buttons*, William Carlos Williams' *Kora in Hell: Improvisations*
(two texts written with a conscious, although not imitative, relation
to the French model in mind), Robert Creeley's *Presences* or *A Day
Book* or John Ashbery's *Three Poems*. *Poets' Prose*[3] by Stephen
Fredman focuses almost entirely on Williams, Creeley and Ashbery.
Major anthologies of American poetry, in general, including ones
by Donald Allen and Hayden Carruth, omit any kind of poetic
prose. Lyn Hejinian's work, *My Life*, is listed by its publisher as a
"short novel," while Kathy Acker's *Great Expectations* was
excerpted as an example of "language poetry" by the French journal
Change. Nor is this confusion necessarily limited to English
literature: *Les Chants de Maldoror*, published one year *prior* to
Baudelaire's "miracle of poetic prose," is called by its English
translator, Alexis Lykiard, "neither novel nor prose-poem," yet is
assigned no other category.

What is it about poetry and prose, and of the mixing of these
modes, which yields such a lack of consensus?

One answer, which has been proposed by Michael Davidson
and is followed by Fredman, argues that a distinction must be made
between "the conventional prose poem" and what Davidson
alternately calls "the new prose," "non- or inter-generic prose
forms" and "the prose of fact." Fredman's term for the larger
terrain is "poet's prose." According to this view, "prose-poetry, in
the conventional sense, is a highly marked form; it has a distinct
tone, rhetoric, and even subject matter involved with it."[4] Thus,
"the conventional prose poem of Robert Bly, James Wright or W.S.

Merwin is scenic; it projects a *paysage moralise*, a landscape upon which is grafted a series of psychological speculations."[5] For Davidson, the term prose poem designates only a narrow portion of the much broader territory between poetry and prose.

This perspective of a wider field of poetic prose might seem to justify the omissions in Benedikt's anthology. It might even account for the inclusion of a reasonably modest French writer of short pieces, such as Geo Norge, while someone who worked primarily in longer (therefore more ambiguous) forms, such as St.-John Perse, is absent. Yet a closer inspection of this collection reveals some interesting contradictions. First, certain authors are represented in a manner consistent with Benedikt's own vision of a highly marked conventional form—regardless of the shape and concerns of their lifework taken as a whole. This is most apparent in the selections of Francis Ponge, whose 14 short pieces in the collection take up only 15 pages. Ponge's major prose works include the complex (but easily excerptible) 97 page *Soap*, and *The Notebook of the Pine Woods*, neither of which is scenic or shares the tone and rhetoric to which Davidson refers. Benedikt's editing implies that there is a fundamental difference, or rupture, between the short pieces and larger works, that they are different genres, and so misrepresents the essential continuity and cohesion of Ponge's work. Yet the "conventional" prose poets in Benedikt's gathering not only lack the homogeneity one might expect of a fixed genre, but the book also includes several authors who certainly did not imagine that they were (at least in these particular pieces) writing poetry: Franz Kafka, Jorge Luis Borges and Julio Cortázar.

Nonetheless, even beyond Benedikt's bias (his inclusions tend toward the overtly narrative while omissions, such as Stein or Williams, do not), Davidson's demand for a distinction between the prose poem and poet's prose is not borne out by the evidence. His assertion is that the prose works of Bly, Wright and Merwin are conventional, and that the conventions are those of *poesis pure*, i.e., the poetics embodied in the writings of Baudelaire, Mallarmé and Valéry. In fact, from the perspective of literary history, the prose poetry of Bly, Ignatow, Merwin et al, the sort of stuff that could be found in any issue of *Kayak*, is an anomaly. The writing of these Americans is conventional only insofar as they, and they alone, desire a standardized, predictable form. In this, they counter the dominant impulse of prose poetry, internationally, since Baudelaire. In its emphasis of the idea of *difference*, of a writing which could never achieve or become its own model, *Paris Spleen* calls into question the very possibility of convention and its founding premise (perhaps the hidden assumption of all literature): the stability, or even existence, of genre.

To know, then, what the prose poem is or might be, we must first ask: what is prose?

Following Davidson, let us begin by noting that it is a word, a noun, derived from the French and that, in turn, from Latin, *proversus*, the past participle of *provertere*, meaning "to turn towards." Thus a single Latin verb lies at the etymological root of both "prose" and "verse," verse coming from the root which meant "to turn" and prose from "towards."

The primary definition given by the *Oxford English Dictionary*, which tells us this, is:

> The ordinary form of written or spoken language, without metrical structure: especially as a species or division of literature. Opposed to *poetry, verse, rime* or *metre.*

This sense of oppositionality, of prose *against* verse, out of roots that had once combined to form a whole, is significant. A character in Molière's *Bourgeois Gentleman* offers a similar equation, in which

Poetry = Prose + a + b + c
Prose = Poetry – a – b – c[6]

Even in this formula we can dimly perceive how such oppositionality may not so much be that of negation as one of the two ends or limits of a continuous spectrum. This model of *linear continuity* is inscribed within, and dominates, most modern presentations of this question. Wordsworth may have been the first to challenge the polarity of this view:

> The only strict antithesis to Prose is Metre; nor is this, in truth a *strict* antithesis, because lines and passages of metre so naturally occur in writing prose, that it would be scarcely possible to avoid them, even were it desirable.[7]

This suggests that all writing is a mixed mode, a motley or patchwork of poetic and prosaic effects, a position which is extended by New Critics René Welleck and Austin Warren, in *Theory of Literature*, into yet another variation of the spectrum paradigm, where the distinction is now merely a matter of degrees:

> The phonetic stratus is a necessary precondition of the meaning. The distinction between a novel by Dreiser and a poem like Poe's "The Bells" is in this and prosaic effects, a position which respect *only quantitative* and fails to justify the setting up of two contrasting kinds of literature, literature, fiction and poetry.[8]

Literature, in the version proposed more recently by Tzvetan Todorov, encompasses the middle of this spectrum:

> In order to define poetry, it is not enough to say how it differs from prose, for the two have a common portion which is literature.[9]

We find this model of a continuum again, in miniature, in the poetics of Louis Zukofsky, defined, in Robert Creeley's words, "as a function, having as lower limit, speech, and upper limit, song."[10]

Zukofsky's scale, in which music, poetry and speech all exist as degrees of intensity of the same phenomenon, for all of its precursors within the history of literature, contrasts sharply with the view put forward by linguist Ferdinand de Saussure:

> Writing, though unrelated to its inner system, is used continually to represent language. We cannot simply disregard it. We must be acquainted with its usefulness, shortcoming, and dangers. . . . *Language and writing are two distinct systems of signs*; the second exists for the sole purpose of representing the first. . . . The first linguists confused language and writing, just as the humanists had done before them. . . . Still today intelligent men confuse language and writing. . . . Writing obscures language; it is not a guise for language but a disguise.[11]

Yet where, for Saussure, "writing assumes undeserved importance," Roman Jakobson, a later practitioner who carried his work in linguistics over into the field of literary theory, arrived at a new paradigm with far different implications:

> Prose—for example, 'oral narrative,' 'practical prose,' 'scientific

writing,' 'journalistic prose,' 'legal discourse,' 'literary' and 'fictional' prose, etc.—is a *transitional phenomenon*, admitting of various gradations on the continuum between 'ordinary' language with an orientation toward the referential function and the poetic function. As a transitional phenomenon, prose evidences a more complex type, a type in which the poetic and referential modes are intertwined in various ways and to varying degrees. 'Literary prose' is, presumably, closer to the poetic end, while 'practical prose' would be closer to the referential end. This means that the 'poetics of prose' and in general the analysis of literary, nonpoetic discourse is more complex than the analysis of either 'true' poetry or of decidedly referential discourse.[12]

Significantly, Jakobson's conceptualization of language and writing is not strictly linear like a radio dial: the referential and poetic are but two of six functions present in any given act of verbal communication:

(1) an Addresser, e.g., a speaker, an author, a narrator;
(2) an Addressee;
(3) a Code, a system, or, to use Saussure's term, a *langue*;
(4) a Message, which is *not* the signified or content, but the *signifier*, Saussure's *parole*, the actual words, the discourse, or text;
(5) a Context, by which Jakobson means a *referent*; and
(6) a Contact, "a physical channel and psychological connection between speaker and addressee."

It is within this framework that Jakobson states

The set toward the message as such, focus on the message for its own sake, is the poetic function of language.[13]

Thus, if an opposition is to be set up between the poetic and referential functions of a communication in order to conceive of this relationship on the model of a continuum or scale, this is because, in "poetic language" (or, better, "the poetic uses of language"), the referent or context *is* the message.

But here, Linda R. Waugh, a collaborator of Jakobson's, warns:

The definition of the poetic function should, as with all statements by Jakobson, be taken as relational: in the poetic function, *in relation to and as against* the five other functions of language, there is a dominance of a focus upon the message. . . . Dominance presumes a hierarchization . . . , not an absolutization. . . . [14]

The assertion of both the relatedness of functions and the essence of the poetic lying in the *message's focus on its own existence* parallels closely this passage by Paul Valéry:

> Walking, like prose, has a definite aim. It is an act directed at something we wish to reach. Actual circumstances . . . , which order the manner of walking, prescribe its direction and its speed, and give it a *definite end*. All the characteristics of walking derive from these instantaneous conditions, which combine *in a novel way* each time. There are no movements in walking that are not special adaptations, but, each time, they are abolished and, as it were, absorbed by the accomplishment of the act, by the attainment of the goal.
>
> The dance is quite another matter. It is . . . a system of actions . . . whose end is in themselves. It goes nowhere. . . .
>
> Here we come again to the contrast between prose and poetry. Prose and poetry use the same words, the same syntax, the same forms, and the same sounds or tones, but differently co-ordinated and differently aroused. . . . But here is the great and decisive difference. When the man who is walking has reached his goal . . . when he has reached the place, book, fruit, the object of his desire . . . , this possession at once entirely annuls his whole act; the effect swallows up the cause, the end absorbs the means; and, whatever the act, only the result remains. It is the same with utilitarian language. . . .
>
> The poem on the other hand, does not die for having lived; it is expressly designed to be born again from its ashes and to become endlessly what it has just been. [15]

Dance does indeed correspond to what Jakobson calls the "poetic function," and not merely ballet or break-dancing, but also a skipping child, the uses of the hands in the "high five" or in a soul handshake. Such activities, which set the focus on the message, on themselves, can be found *throughout the entire range of body movements*. If we attempt to extend Valéry's analogy further, so as to locate the place of "writing" (and, through this, "prose") within this terrain, the history of contemporary choreography and Laban notation demonstrate not merely the possibility of a performative script, but also that nothing with the range of feasible human motions need be excluded from the dancer's repertoire. In this sense, even the silent sitting of the Buddhist in meditation, attention turned entirely to the most minute issues of posture and breathing, constitutes a demonstration of the "poetic function." Orientation within the communicative act between the six functions thus appears to be primarily a matter of intention or self-awareness. Such would be the distinction between the clerical worker "mindlessly" placing files in alphabetical order and the Theravada monk performing the same task while conducting "working meditation."

It is just this latency of the poetic function within any text that led Valéry's mentor, Stephane Mallarmé, to upend Baudelaire's original dream entirely, denying the very existence of prose:

> Verse is everywhere in language where there is rhythm; everywhere, except in advertisements and on the fourth page of the newspapers. In the genre referred to as prose there are verses, sometimes admirable ones, of all kinds of rhythm. But, in truth, there is no prose: there is the alphabet, and then there is verse, more or less tightened, more or less diffuse. Everytime there is an effort toward style, then there is versification.[16]

This whimsical declaration (which, in spite of its conclusion, echoes Wordsworth) fails to anticipate Saussure's later assertion that writing and language are distinct systems of signs. If, in fact, this distinction were the case, then, between the "poetic function" of *language* outlined by Jakobson and the actual genre of *writing* known to us as poetry (including the prose poem), there would exist an insurmountable breach. This rupture would be writing itself, the intervention of an implement, be it goose quill or word processor, the fact of the alphabet.

This breach, if real, would invalidate forever any model of language and literature in the form of an unbroken continuum or spectrum. No one has done more to bring attention to this possiblity than Jacques Derrida, whose primary concern has not been the categories of linguistics, literature or criticism, but rather a desire to refute what he terms the "logocentric metaphysics" that function as the basis of all western thought. Consequently, this *de*constructionist offers an anti-paradigm, of sorts, in which writing is neither reduced to a mere guise or graphic representation of speech, nor separated out from it as a "distinct system of signs."

Rather, writing and speech are joined, so that the "gap," that incommensurable aspect which first caused Saussure to propose his distinction, serves instead to "fatally flaw" any hoped for, or assumed, unity of meaning within whatever this larger construct might be. Derrida's name for this greater entity, an index of just how revolutionary he wishes his thought to be, is *writing*, not language.

Derrida's argument is that for writing to have come into existence it must have been possible, and therefore implicit, within language. Furthermore, writing, as Saussure said of spelling, "influences and modifies language." Had Derrida gone this far and perhaps no further, then it might have been feasible to extend these insights toward a positive "science" of writing, a portion of which would include the answers to our questions concerning the prose poem. Derrida himself calls for such a practice, naming it *grammatology*—yet it is not possible to proceed from his work in the direction of this discipline.

Part of the problem lies in the ethics of Derrida's method. The site of this fundamental breach in all western metaphysics, between presence, being and life on the one side, and absence, non-being and death on the other, is said to be fixed precisely in the distinction between phoneme and grapheme. For Derrida, the metaphysical importance of the phoneme lies in the fact that its speaker must hear it *within* her body as it is spoken, present to her, unified. Conversely, the grapheme is the arch-figure of absence, alienation, death. If the systems of writing and language, of grapheme and phoneme, are indissolubly joined, absence is seen to inhabit presence and there can exist no beingness uninfected by non-being, no living which is not, in the same instant, dead. From this, Derrida argues that the western tradition of rational method and the hope for a knowable world are nothing more than the twin sides of a sustained, monstrous hoax: the logic of presence is predicated upon a denial of death. All that is really attainable is partial insight into the fundamental operations of difference (a term Derrida pays homage to by spelling it *differance*), through which all signifieds, all meanings, exist. By announcing this breach while still joining writing to speech, Derrida raises the "pure negativity" of the phoneme to the status of law, *differance*, arguing in the same moment against the unity of this system.

The circularity of his thesis is no accident. If positive

knowledge is not possible, what remains is the endless play of distinctions. Attempting to demonstrate that Saussure's banishment of writing from the field fundamentally undermines linguistics' claim to be a "scientific" discourse, Derrida writes:

> Linguistics . . . wishes to be the science of language. . . . Let us first simply consider that the scientificity of that science is often acknowledged because of its *phonological* foundations. Phonology, it is often said today, communicates its scientificity to linguistics, which in turn serves as the epistemological model for all the sciences of man. Since the deliberate and systematic phonological orientation of linguistics (Troubetzkoy, Jakobson, Martinet) carries out an intention which was originally Saussure's, I shall, at least provisionally, confine myself to the latter.[17]

If, as he argues, the "scientificity" of phonology *as practiced by Saussure* is the key to the "epistemological model for all the sciences of man," then a great deal is riding on there being a homology between Saussure's own theory of the phonetic realm and that used by subsequent linguists, such as Jakobson.

This identity does not exist.

Although Derrida treats Saussure's *Course in General Linguistics* as a unified work, it is in fact a compilation made after his death of material presented in three classes over a five year period. The editors relied on the notebooks of seven students and a single notation taken by an eighth.

Writing in 1943, Jakobson noted:

> The *Course in General Linguistics* contains serious contradictions in its manner of understanding and describing the phonic resources of language. . . . In the section of the *Course* on phonology these contradictions were magnified by the editors, who themselves later expressed their regret at having mechanically collected together Saussure's notes on phonology, since they did in fact derive from very different stages of his scientific work. for example, in chapter VII of the Introduction we find an unqualified identification of phonology with the physiology of sounds, and yet a few lines later Saussure asserts that 'what is important in analysis' is not 'the movements of the vocal apparatus which are necessary for the production of each acoustic image', but solely the operation of the oppositions which are put to work by language.[18]

It is just such internal inconsistencies which empower Derrida's assault on Saussure, but which he sees not as the consequence of an imperfect editing project so much as the tell-tale sign of a fundamental flaw, the banishment of writing from the field of linguistics. The theory of *differance* hinges on the acceptance by linguists (and specifically the structuralists) of the Saussurean "thesis of *differance* as the source of linguistic value," which is what enables Derrida to submit the elements of writing to the pure negativity of the phoneme. Here again, Jakobson is unmistakably clear:

> Whereas all other elements have *specific, positive content, direct meaning*, phonemes by contrast have a solely differential value, thus a purely negative value. . . . Saussure understood the purely differential and negative character of phonemes perfectly well, but instead of drawing out the implications of this for the analysis of the phoneme he *overhastily generalized* this characterization and sought to apply it to all linguistic entities. He went so far as to assert that there are in language only differences with no positive terms. . . . Now on this point Saussure committed the serious mistake of confusing two different ideas. Grammatical categories are relative entities, and their meanings are determined by the whole system of categories of a given language, and by the play of oppositions within this system. For example, it is obvious that the grammatical category of the plural presupposes and implies the existence of an opposite category, that of the singular. But what is crucial for the plural category, what legitimates its existence in the language, is its own positive value, i.e., the designation of a plurality. . . . All opposition of grammatical categories necessarily has a positive content, whereas the opposition of two phonemes never has.[19]

There are two problems here, only one of which is Derrida's falsification of the record. If his grammatological scheme collapses because the evidence is tainted, the question still remains as to the status of writing with regard to language, and, within this, that of the phoneme to the grapheme. A positive science of writing, within which we might hope to clarify our own small issue of prose and the prose poem, has yet to be brought forward.

It is here that the inconsistencies in Saussure's approach cause genuine methodological difficulties. If writing "obscures" and "is not a guise . . . but a disguise" for language, then the structure and function of this mask would appear to lie *outside* the linguistic realm. Jakobson's attempt at a rectification of the Saussurean project returns writing to language, but only as a secondary category, predicated upon a defense of the status of the phoneme:

> In characterising phonemes as differential and negative entities, Saussure was led to declare that an identical state of affairs exists in that other sign system, writing. He held that "the value of letters is purely negative and differential. . . . " But the thing which is of primary significance here is the specific, positive value of each grapheme. Of course the letter *beta* must be distinguished from the letters *alpha, gamma, delta,* etc., but the *raison d'etre* for the Greek grapheme *beta* is its designation of the phoneme *b,* and all the other graphemes have a similar task to perform. The graphic image functions as a signifier and the phoneme as its signified.[20]

This oversimplifies a much more complex relationship, arriving at a conclusion which can be disproven. There are, just to cite the English language, more phonemes than graphemes or letters. Following the work of William Haas, Johanna Drucker argues:

> A single grapheme may be rendered by any one of several phonemes (as in the case of (c): license, cat) or vice versa, a single phoneme may be rendered by different graphemes (xylophone, zygote). The graphemes do not bear a one-to-one unalterable relation with phonemes, and the sounds and letters are related by correspondence, not by reference. For letters to "stand for" sounds it would be necessary to consider them the signs of phonemes. . . . Graphemes may be, in most cases but not all, translated into phonemes and vice versa, but this is a translation process, these are essentially two different language systems and a rough correspondence exists between them which is generally sufficient to permit the change from one form to the other to take place. The specifics of accent and emphasis and timing are missing from most conventional written transcriptions of spoken utterance; on the other hand, there are conventions in writing which do not translate into speech. . . . [21]

Individual graphemes, like phonemes, function in a primarily negative and differential manner, utilizing the features of position, orientation, number of strokes, and size or degree of extension. In groups ("words"), graphemes refer not to phonemes, but to the language itself. Individually, the grapheme *b* refers to a word in the language, the name of a letter. Even when grapheme "stands for" a phoneme, what it represents is that phoneme's existence in the language *as a word*. If, historically, some alphabets began as representation of phonemic systems, this function was a convention soon subverted by the reality that any mode of *parole* is a fluid, fragile and partial manifestation of the *langue*. Writing, therefore, is no more a disguise for language than is speech. Saussure was correct in stating that writing "exists for the sole purpose of representing" language, but only insofar as the same is true for speech. Each is a representation, a manifestation, a *parole*. Writing and speaking are not joined, even as portrayed in the Derridean counter-model, but are separate systems with important differences. They are possessed, and utilized, by literate persons in much the same way that a bilingual individual might have access to, say, Huichol and Spanish. Because they are learned *interactively*—a school child demonstrates knowledge of a new word by her ability to both say and spell it—any recognition of distinctions between the two systems is minimized: each is subsumed by a common referent, the *langue*.

If writing and speaking are overlapping, but not identical, subsets of a greater whole, where might the differences be that give rise, in writing, to prose, and hence to the prose poem? The relative mobility and permanence of a text versus that of the speech act, the "recent" origin of writing itself (Derrida's obfuscations notwithstanding) and the still limited reach of literacy, are commonplaces here. Certainly the tendency toward hypotaxis in writing and toward parataxis in speech—a distinction deserving much greater investigation—leads inexorably through the history of the European languages to the hierarchically organized expository essay as the model written discourse, what Barthes refers to as "classical language."

But, perhaps as critical as any of these in creating a ground for the prose poem is a tendency within each *parole* to mimic the other, particularly in areas affected by social and/or class constraints. Thus "refined" speech is consciously patterned after the hypotactic organization of writing, while students of the "high" discourse of "creative" writing are often instructed to put down their thoughts "as if you were speaking." That this mimetic impulse is never sufficient to represent the opposing *parole* may be less important

106

than the simple existence of an Other from which to discover, and on which to model, the possibility of stylization itself.

It is at this point that I would place the origin of Baudelaire's "miracle of a poetic prose," first in France and, due to a displacement which demonstrates precisely these dynamics, more recently in the United States. This "miracle" is nothing less than a recognition of the possibility of the transcendence of genre, that dimension without which the "problem" of the prose poem would pose no difficulty at all. Both the tendency of writing, as a *parole*, toward the hierarchic compartmentalizations of the hypotactic, and the increased permanence and influence of the text, render the graphic representation of language more vulnerable to organization by fixed categories than is the case with speech. While this reached the point of unconscious self-parody in the restrictions imposed by the French Academy by the early 19th century, the claustrophobia that resulted from generic and stylistic prohibitions was felt in Britain as well: one need only read Alexander Pope to sense where hypotaxis in verse might lead.

The advent of modernism in France, Baudelaire's "accident," was paralleled by a turn on the part of English-speaking poets toward a different analysis of the problem, and thereby a different solution. If the French glimpsed, however briefly and incompletely, the possibility of a practice that, transcending the constraints of writing, would lead back from *parole* to *langue*, the British instead proceed from one *parole* to the other, toward speech. The English equivalent to Baudelaire's dedication to Houssaye is, in this sense, Wordsworth's "Preface" to the second edition of *Lyrical Ballads*. Ironically, the term Wordsworth chooses to identify the plain-speaking of the common person, his paradigm for direct communication as opposed to the closed categories of verse, is *prose*. Six decades before *Paris Spleen*, he writes:

> The language of Prose may yet be well adapted to Poetry; and . . . a large portion of the language of every good poem can in no respect differ from that of good Prose. We will go further. It may be safely affirmed, that there neither is, nor can be, any *essential* difference between the language of prose and metrical composition.[22]

Wordsworth perceived the constraints imposed on poetry by the tendencies within writing toward closure, but failed to connect that element of hierarchic organization with the inner-workings of prose itself. Incorporating prose dynamics into verse structures exactly reverses the direction of the prose poem's thrust while retaining its basic components. Nearly two centuries later, this same perspective still dominates normative Anglo-American poetry. The Pound-Williams tradition, a counter-poetics which evolved in response to hypotactic constraints on 20th century American verse, can itself be read as an argument over emphasis within the same framework proposed by Wordsworth. Rather than posing the question as to why Wordsworth's approach had come to a dead end, these "more modernist" poets sought only to upgrade his tactics, developing poetic forms that accurately represented the paratactic organization of the speech chain.

Yet, it was from within this oppositional poetics that the new prose, or prose poem, appeared. By equating the free verse line with the quantity of speaking that could occur between two pauses for breath, Charles Olson in 1950 made available an enormously refined system for scoring the habits of dialect and idiolect on the printed page. However, once an adequate depiction of an individual's speech was possible, the limits which this strategy offered as to what could then be written became clear. Thus it was Robert Grenier, writing in the first issue of *This*, who announced the desire to

> for our time proclaim an abhorrence of 'speech' designed as was [Williams'] castigation of the 'the sonnet' to rid us, as creators of the world, from reiteration of the past dragged on in formal habit. I HATE SPEECH.[23]

The writing envisioned in the hyperbole of those capitalized letters shares with Baudelaire's "miracle" the intention of a project capable of going beyond the constraints not merely of its genre and literary allegiances, but beyond those of its own *parole*. As such, it seeks not to reinsert the hypotactic organization of classical prose, and certainly not to confine the paratactic to an idealization of speaking, but to call forth the possibilities within both dimensions so as to make full use of that which is their shared referent, the language itself.

MIGRATORY MEANING

In the Spring/Summer 1981 issue of *Parnassus*, Peter Schjeldahl has this to say of *Transmigration Solo* by Joseph Ceravolo:

> Ceravolo is a lyric poet of such oddness and purity that reading him all but makes me dizzy, like exercise at a very high altitude. *I rarely know what he is talking about*, but I can rarely gainsay a word he uses. Nor do I doubt that every word is in felt contact with actual experience *beyond the experience of words*. He is quite old-fashioned in this way, though so original that it's easy to miss, easy to imagine a new-fangled abstraction . . . . In this relatively early work he had not quite achieved the crystalline timbre of his later poetry, but you can't possibly mistake it for someone else's. Already there is the dominance of usages I want to call "off" or "bent," like vamped notes in jazz. (emphasis added)[1]

Schjeldahl's vocabulary and tone are strategic, both with regard to the audience to which it is addressed, and to that ultimate editorial arbiter, space. I doubt that he intends to be read quite as literally as I am about to suggest. Nevertheless, his piece suggests that not comprehending what a poet "is talking about" should *not* be an impediment to appreciation and response. And, further, that his reaction to Ceravolo is founded on a trust that there exists "beyond the experience of words" a unified, unitary signification or objective correlative—he calls it "contact with actual experience"—which governs the individual poem's impression of coherence.

These two assertions reflect the currect situation in much of American poetry. There persists the lack of an adequate shared vocabulary with which to think and speak of the poem as we find it, circa 1982—to the degree that someone as qualified and predisposed to read one as Peter Schjeldahl is prepared to praise in public work in which he admits not knowing what the poet "is talking about." This obscures precisely what is at risk in those writings which I find most compelling—the nature of meaning itself, and its status in the poem. Specifically, the issue is a question as to the alleged capacity of meaning to unify a work of writing, to create and endow coherence, whether or not this be conceived of as "beyond the experience of words" or within them.

One such poem, as given by Schjeldahl in his review, is Ceravolo's "Migratory Moon":

> Cold and the cranes.
> Cranes in the
>   wind
> like cellophane tape
> on a school book.
> The wind bangs
> the car, but I sing out loud,
>   help, help
> as sky gets white
>   and whiter and whiter and whiter.
> Where are you
>   in the reincarnate
>   blossoms of the cold?[2]

"Migratory Moon" can be said to consist of five parts, a title and four sentences, no two of which coinhabit the same line. By focusing on the sentence, the poem can be described as a *series of devices* both simple and complex. Device is used here in the Russian Formalists' sense: any part of the writing which perceptibly alters, and thereby shapes, an individual reader's experience of the text.[3]

The title is not a sentence, but simply an alliterative noun phrase, neither term of which occurs in the body of the text. It could be either the subject *or* predicate of a sentence which does not appear, but can be said *to have been evoked.* The phrase performs the work of both grammatical functions, doubling the sense of density or opacity to a reader.

It's important to discern whether "Migratory Moon" functions principally as a title or, following a distinction first made by Walter Benjamin[4], is really more of a caption. A title proper points or refers to the body of the text as a whole, whereas the caption *penetrates* it, highlighting certain elements within. This often occurs in poems where the title anticipates or repeats *in advance* key terms or phrases.

A more complex instance of title-as-caption is to be found in this work by Robert Grenier:

THREE
legged dog[5]

"Three" integrates grammatically with a potentially incomplete noun phrase to form a full image, specifically one of imbalance. "Three" also foretells the number of syllables in the one-line text, again an imbalance, as the ear hears the stress given to the final syllable in "legged." This title penetrates the text not simply to foreground one element, but to combine with it for the total organization of the poem. Implicit within such a strategy is an assertion that "meaning" does not stop conveniently at the borders of the text.

Contrasted with this would be those titles which at least appear to have no *inner* role within the poem. Examples include Barrett Watten's "Mode Z" and Eliot's "The Waste Land." Such headings can only be read as though relating to the body of the work as a whole, so that the reader experiences them as orienting and contextualizing, if not actually naming, the "subject" of the ensuing text.

"Migratory Moon" would at first seem to be such a title. Without explicit references to it in the text, the reader has only her own authority on which to rely if the moon is to be identified with the "you" of the final sentence. Nonetheless, at this stage of our reading, we do seem to know what Ceravolo "is talking about": the moon. Yet "Migratory Moon," is at least partially a case of the title-as-caption, and, as such, prompts a leap of faith that allows the reader to experience a cohering unity.

Like the title, the first sentence is grammatically incomplete. If we follow speech act theory in arguing that the characteristic of a subject is its capacity to intend, or refer to, a unique object, and that of a predicate is the ability to "describe or characterize the object which has been identified,"[6] we still lack any mechanism by which to ascertain which, if either, function "Cold and the cranes" fulfills. It could indicate an object or state, yet its proximity to "Migratory Moon" permits a reading of the title as subject, and this fragmentary first sentence as an attribute of it.

Sentences which are incomplete because of the lack of a "main" verb have long been a part of American literature. One version of this tradition descends from Imagism, particularly the work of Ezra Pound. As Hugh Kenner notes, Pound's model for "In a Station of the Metro" was the Japanese haiku.[7]

In "Cold and the cranes," the omission ambiguously situates what little information is divulged. The important terms are nouns, one of which is plural (a disagreement in number that may suggest that more than one verb is absent). Both nouns have more than one feasible denotation, and nothing in the text clarifies whether these cranes are mechanical arms that lift and carry, or birds. This indetermination keeps the reader from knowing what Ceravolo "is talking about," at one level, but at another makes no difference, since neither crane is apt to inhabit the indoors. This *outdoorsness* is an example of what some linguists call a *frame* or *schema*, and "represent(s) the knowledge structures with which or experiences with the world are held together,"[8] that is, what we know and can associate with cranes or with *the* cold, head colds and the like. This association significantly narrows each noun's range of connotation. "Moon" likewise fits this frame, so that without having arrived at a single verb, and before reaching even the second line, a sensitive reader is well on the way toward the construction of what linguists Charles Fillmore and Paul Kay call an *Envisionment*,

some coherent 'image' or understanding of the states of affairs that exist in the set of possible worlds compatible with the language of the text.[9]

Harboring a metaphor of sight that needs detailed examination, Envisionment is a less-than-ideal critical construct. Yet it does help us approach our problem: At this moment in "Migratory Moon" *outdoorsness* seems to result less from "felt contact" than from a series of devices operating in the work. This is not to denigrate the poem, but to suggest that the experience of contact and unity is not beyond the experience of words at all, but is itself just an effect.

A theory of Envisionment offers above the level of the sentence what other forms of linguistic analysis offer at or below this horizon: identification and description by function of those devices which create meaning. Meaning is built on all levels upon expectation, and that on experience, be it as large as "life in general" or as localized as the title and first line of "Migratory Moon."

By displacing expectation, the semantic shift renders the

element "strange" and therefore perceptible. Shklovsky's account of this is:

> the artistic . . . is purposely created to deautomatize the perception, . . . the goal of its creation is that it be seen, . . . so that perception is arrested in it and attains the greatest possible force and duration, so that the thing is perceived, not spatially, but, so to speak, in its continuity. . . . Thus we arrive at the definition of poetry as speech that is braked, distorted. Poetic speech is a speech construction.[10]

The emphasis on time, contrasted with the spatial, reflects the importance of expectation in the creation of meaning in writing. The effect of a semantic shift is therefore both experiential *and* temporal.

The shifts which exist in the title, "Migratory Moon," are modest and result from devices well known to readers of poetry. (Alliteration, for example, foregrounds the sound structure.) More problematic is the adjective "Migratory," a term for which plausible frames exist that could integrate with those of "Moon." To what degree can we believe that these are the ones intended, let alone sort among variants such as the moon's daily cycle, its drift north and south, its phases, the effect on tides, the mythos of wanderlust, lunacy, etc? Charles Fillmore identifies what he terms *levels of confidence* in Envisionment, degrees to which the reader can be sure that her interpretation is the one, and only one, intended by the author. Fillmore delineates four levels:

(1) that which is "explicitly justified by the linguistic material of the text;"

(2) that which comes "into being by inferences which the text is seen as clearly inviting;"

(3) "interpretations which result from schematizations *brought* to the text to situate its events in common experience;" and

(4) "ways in which the world of the text has been shaped by the idiosyncratic experience and imaginings of individual readers."[11]

Envisionments in poetry depend on these different degrees of confidence, which are in fact *levels of importation* of detail and nuance.

An anecdote here may convey some sense of their power and function. In my seminar at San Francisco State, we were discussing a work by Rae Armantrout, "Grace," a short poem in three sections, each of which, for the purposes of this discussion, can be said to embody the title concept. Here is the first section:

a spring there
where his entry must be made

signals him on[12]

Three differing Envisionments were offered to account for the passage, a process close to Ludwig Wittgenstein's proposition that "meaning is what an explanation of meaning explains."[13]
In the first, a diver was about to enter a swimming pool, the spring found in the resilience of the diving board. In the second, an actor was about to go onstage, and the spring in his or her first step was vital in creating the spirit, the literal, physical rhythm of the role. In the third, a person was attempting to enter a forest or climb a mountain, but was blocked, unable to make progress until a spring opened up a path. All three present narrative scenarios, schematizations imported into the reading so as to contextualize its terms, particularly "spring" and "entry" (the subjects, respectively, of the host and embedded sentences). Note that the third Envisionment, which seems fanciful, defines "spring" as a flow of liquid, rather than as a bouncy quality. This parallels Armantrout's own authorial Envisionment, that of vaginal lubrication.

That her version should be no more "explicitly justified" by the text is not surprising. In "7 Days in Another Town," Kit Robinson presents a ten line poem accompanied by a letter "explaining" the work image by image, line by line. Here is his discourse on the first stanza, "Mesopotamian wind/blows the same way twice:"

Mesopotamian for the UniRoyal plant with its incredible Sargon of Akkhad design. Also for Griffith's depiction of Babylonian Intolerance & the fact that LA, like that metropolitan area, was settled by nomads who had to come across the desert.
Wind for that gale that nearly blew us off our feet & made walking to the bank an adventure.
Blows the same way twice (in fact, "forever") in Topanga Canyon where we saw aisles of stone raked up the sides of hills by the air off eons & crouched in curved saucer-shaped caves carved out by same—

twice in contrapunction to remark of Heraclitus about not being to step in same river any more times than one, his point being a universal state of flux, whereas in LA forms tend toward a monolithic eternal Idea, like the movies, or Century City isn't about to budge.[14]

This demonstrates a literal "felt contact with actual experience the experience beyond of words," yet Robinson's concern here is not to create a vision of unity for the reader, at least not in the sense of closure and simple determinancy. The meaning of the writing cannot be located "beyond," but only constructed through its actual elements *combined with* experiences of the reader. It is, as Jackson Mac Low argues, "perceiver-centered."[15]

What renders the phrase "Migratory Moon" problematic, accounts for the varying Envisionments in "Grace," and which is addressed, perhaps even challenged, in "7 Days in Another Town," is the *Parsimony Principle*. Like Envisionment, frame and schema, this is a concept appropriated from the work of linguists concerned with elaborating a theory of ideal readers, one of whom is posited to exist for each given text,

> someone who knows, at each point in a text, everything that the text presupposes at that point, and who does not know, but is prepared to receive and understand, what the text introduces at that point.[16]

The Parsimony Principle converts the latency of the text and the ideological dimensions of presupposition into an actual Envisionment, combining frames always to a maximum of unification with a minimum of effort. It can be defined:

> whenever it is possible to integrate two separate schema into a single larger frame-structure *by imagining them as sharing a common participant* the reader will do so.[17]

This is what enables some readers to discover narratives in poem after poem of Bruce Andrews. It is what empowers anyone to conclude that "The Waste Land" names or has any other relation beyond mere physical proximity to a text by Eliot, one that was originally entitled "He Do the Police in Different Voices." The Parsimony Principle is the process through which, to adopt the terminology of Alan Davies and Nick Piombino, we "connect the dots."[18]

There is *no* device which explicitly determines the appropriate frame for "Migratory." Insofar as whooping cranes do migrate, the title proposes, momentarily, that envisionment. However, industrial cranes are a part of urban lifestyle, a schema that can incorporate "cars" and "cellophane tape/on a school book" as *Grus americana* cannot. The envisionment is both set up and countered, each step in this process displacing expectation.

The disagreement in number between "cold" and "the cranes" suggests not only that more than one verb might be missing, but also that this phrase may be an asymmetrical fragment of a larger formulation—for instance, "I'm cold and the cranes are hovering." But it is also possible to construct a frame sentence in which "Cold" is plural and only a single main verb needed, e.g., "We are cold and the cranes colder." However, several devices within the poem argue against this: the asymmetry of the conjunction's placement; the plural-to-singular movement of the second sentence; and the use of "cold" in the poem's last line. What might have been the simplest construction evoked by the first line is thus blocked by the development of the poem.

Another major device is to be found in the use of conjunctions: "and" in the first sentence, "like" in the second, "but" and the multiple occurrences of "and" in the third. Prepositions also bring lexical items together. In nine of the thirteen lines one or the other is used to express a relationship between terms. These categories ascribe such relations even when verbs are absent—instances where they function as propositions in which the actor making the assertion remains hidden. As novelists have known for more than a century, it is the invisible narrator whom readers find the most difficult to resist.

"Like cellophane tape/on a school book" may be the first semantic shift so pronounced as to be noticeable. "Like," is the most active of coordinate words, marking as does no other conjunction the presence of a point-of-view. It carries within itself the shadow of a speaker, enabling reader resistance. This impediment is intended: the schema to which we are being led will *not* integrate into any frame that could have been constructed from the information thus far received.

This event is not instantaneous, but occurs in time, in the

continual *revision* of expectation. At "cellophane tape," the reader must recognize the shift demanded of her envisionment, yet "on a school book" transforms this, yielding a new *and competing* envisionment. This new one exploits the reader's experience of "cellophane tape/on a school book." The meaningful aspect of this schema, the engine of its humor—and it is funny—, is its "triviality." The social sources of this are several. First, such tape on a book is apt to be nearly invisible, an opposition to its sharpness as a verbal construction. Next is a social convention which holds that what is important about a book is not its binding, and even less so a patchwork repair. Third is the social place of a text specifically intended for use in school and our response and associations to such an object. This element will vary with each person, contributing to its density and "authenticity." For example, it could signify books which are large, physically heavy, poorly written and costly, therefore better purchased in a "used" condition. Last is a much more controversial social convention holding that students themselves are an unproductive, and thus trivial, segment of society. Ceravolo's interest in this question is unclear (and in any event unimportant). Its symmetry with the function of the image *as a device* is what calls it into play, adding to the tension of the larger envisionment. In this way ideological conflicts are built into even the most apolitical of images "like cellophane tape/on a school book."

By the time the reader reaches "The wind bangs," she should be so oriented to the undulating, convoluting sequence of semantic shifts as to viscerally feel the poem's first verb. "The wind" returns us to an earlier stage of the work, recalling the previous frame of outdoorsness. The repetition of the noun implies that each sentence is so separate as to make the backwards-pointing anaphoric function of pronouns pointless. Foregrounding the sentence-as-unit renders the language braked and distorted, while setting up the coming use of reiteration in the last line as the moment of completion.

As a device, "the car" adds to (and revises) the earlier envisionment. It follows the frame of outdoorsness, but within a context of human activity, with no relation to whooping birds, yet capable in itself of a migration.

A transformative moment, this seventh line is different from those which came before, continuing beyond a comma and through a conjunction. "But" is also a kind of negation of what could have been a complete sentence. A narrator is introduced, as is a new schema: singing out loud. The acknowledgement of the speaking subject, "I," comes in the precise middle of the middle line of the poem, equidistant from either use of the term "cold." Structurally elegant though this is, a more important device is the conjuction's function as a disclaimer, which serves to throw the entire relation of cause-and-effect in this text-world into a state of strangeness. At this point the reader may begin to suspect that she will never know what the poet here "is talking about."

And "help, help" doesn't, contrasting a cry for assistance with the frame of singing. Whether this formal inappropriateness is a part of the device or not is problematic, insofar as the punctuation surrounding this embedded cry also ascribes quietness, an equally unsuitable (semantically shifted) quality. Nor, without knowing the date of composition, is it possible to know whether any allusion to the Beatles may be intended.

The following line returns us to the outdoors. "Sky" is a frame which can include the moon, an object perceived as white. It is here, and only within this and the next line, that the narrower, more "concrete" schema *moon* seems fully warranted. In this penetration of the text the title functions as a caption. It links up with these lines to develop a frame suggesting that what is addressed and identified as "you" might be the moon. Again, however, there are as many reasons to conclude that this is not the case. The schematization *moon* is weak in comparison to the more consistent outdoorsness. The radical separateness of previous sentences and the shift in form of address here undermine confidence in the continuity of focus. Finally, "where are you" is senseless if asked of the moon while the "sky gets white/and whiter and whiter and whiter," unless the reader superimposes some association such as snow. Like "cellophane tape/on a school book," the intervention of the title here sets up a competing envisionment not to be resolved.

That the "you" has no identifiable signified, that "you" is, literally, absent, is the thrust of the question: where, under such circumstances, are you? Beyond the moon, one possible response might be that "you" is an Other, specifically a lover. While this interpretation situates the poem well within the lyric subgenre of the "lover's lament," it requires an importation of meaning which rests entirely on a knowledge of literary conventions extraneous to the text.

If the poem is read as turning on, or even completing itself with the word "you," the remaining lines serve only to provide closure. Yet the enjambed phrase "reincarnate/blossoms" goes beyond such a modest function. "Reincarnate" is a term that fits a *Migratory* schema. It also contains the word "car," the long *a* of "cranes," and even an allophonic scramble of the word "crane." "Blossoms" adds one last complicating supplement to the frame of outdoorsness, stressing a pastoral envisionment which recalls that of the first three lines. Even if "reincarnate" were linked directly to "Migratory" it is unlikely that any narrower frame than *the seasons* would result. Rather, "reincarnate" serves as a tease, and "blossoms" as a final component to a complex, unstable whole *not equal* to any single envisionment.

What then is there about this text that a reader like Schjeldahl might not know what the writer "is talking about?"

(1) An unstable—or, better, *destabilized*—total envisionment;
(2) key terms which resist specificity, such as "cranes" and "you";
(3) evidence that the title does not "name" the poem as a whole, but functions instead as a caption;
(4) a seeming rejection of anaphoric connection between sentences.

Given this, what is there about this text that a reader might not "doubt that every word is in felt contact with actual experience beyond the experience of words?" The outdoors schema combined with the perceptible determination of every device. Even those elements, such as "cellophane tape," which resist integration into the dominant frame-structure, bear by their very opposition a relation to it, "felt contact," so that *the whole can be said to determine every device*, insinuating unity and closure.

The degree to which this coherence is a direct consequence of the Parsimony Principle acting *within the mind of the reader* and not the simple determinism of the text can be gauged by the fact that "Migratory Moon" is *not* the title of Ceravolo's poem, but the result of a typographic error. The word in *Transmigration Solo* is "Noon." A single letter transforms the work. The implictions of events such as the cold or the whitening of the sky are changed radically, while "Migratory" itself takes on a new spectrum of possible connotations, that of time passing and of the difference in hour from zone to zone. Yet, like the competing envisionments of the first section of Armantrout's "Grace," there is a limit. Of the four answers given to the first of our questions with regard to the text in *Parnassus*, only one need be altered: "Migratory Noon" is not a caption; nothing within the poem is open to such a penetration. The two versions arrive at dissimilar unifications, each arguing a contact "easily felt."

What can be drawn from this as a contribution towards an eventual shared vocabulary for poets and readers of the contemporary poem? First, that essential to such a lexicon would be a *theory of the device*. Such devices can best be determined and described *by function*, by the shifts which they create in the semantics of the poem, so as, in turn, to demonstrate the contribution of each part to the construction of the whole, whether that be the single envisionment of a vulgarly "realist" text or something more problematic and complex. Without a theory of the device, there can be no rhetoric or listing of those actually in use.

Central to such a theory would be a description of what occurs, both on the page and within the reader, within the infinitesimal space of a semantic shift in relation to the Parsimony Principle, restated here for its broadest application:

> whenever it is possible to integrate two separate elements into a single larger element by imagining them as sharing a common participant, the reader will do so.

One area of further articulation of the Parsimony Principle would be to establish at a finer level of discrimination the degrees of experiential importation which are required at any moment in a text, and to develop the relationship between this process of applying social frames to linguistic material, and the still embryonic theory of ideology which has come from the work of Louis Althusser, Göran Therborn and others.[19] The ideological component within a given work of written art needs to be examined within three separate frames: the instrumental one of "content;" the more dynamic frames of form, genre and *ecriture*; and that of the social construction of experiential schema themselves. The relationships between these realms of signification should also be investigated.

One distinction which needs to be made before a roster of existing devices can be elaborated is the degree to which a procedure can be said to be the same or different when it occurs at different levels of integration—particularly above and below the linguistic horizon of the sentence. This is perhaps most clearly demonstrated by devices aimed precisely at resisting integration itself. Thus "cellophane tape/on a school book," which evades the outdoorsness frame through its lack of any experiential component which is necessarily shared by that schema, is, at the level of the phrase, not unlike Tolstoy's superstructural use of a horse as the narrator for a story, Viktor Shklovsky's classic example of the literary device.[20] Similarly, on a much finer level of distinction, the method through which John Ashbery constructs the first line of "Leaving the Atocha Station" ("The arctic honey blabbed over the report causing darkness"[21]) is through the substitution of three terms which share nothing with an envisionment set up by a more ordinary English sentence, such as "The arctic sun passed over the horizon causing darkness."

Even if we are to grant these the status of a single device, could we in turn distinguish this from other forms of resistance to integration not based on the failure to share experiential frames? This is a distinction which Noam Chomsky attempts to make when he contrasts "colorless green ideas sleep furiously," a string he describes as "grammatical," but "thoroughly meaningless and nonsignificant," with the same words in reverse order, "furiously sleep ideas green colorless."[22] According to Chomsky, "a speaker of English," confronted with the first string,

> will normally read it with the standard intonation pattern of an English sentence. But given some permutation of the words . . . from back to front . . . , he will read it with the intonation pattern characteristic of a list of unrelated words, each with a falling intonation.[23]

Chomsky's example has some close cousins in recent poetry. Bob Perelman's "Alone" in "Cupid & Psyche" reverses "Pleasure" from the same sequence.[24] Charles Bernstein's "So really not visit a remember to strange" is partly a reversal of "As if the Trees by Their Very Roots Had Hold of Us."[25] The resistance to normal syntactic integration occurs because syntax, like time, is essentially unidirectional. Chomsky's explanation is that the only thing we can say directly is that the speaker has an "intuitive sense of grammaticalness."[26]

But is this "intuitive sense" not also an experiential frame?

Is the device of reversed syntax the same as the juxtaposition of larger, non-integrating syntactic units, such as occurs in Lyn Hejinians's *Writing is an Aid to Memory*?[27] Is it the same or different if the point of non-integration takes place at a linebreak as when it happens in the middle of a traditionally punctuated paragraph, as in Kit Robinson's "Fast Howard?"[28] In fact, isn't non-integration and the shifting of semantics at the level of grammar precisely what punctuation attempts to articulate, perhaps even to obliterate, through convention? Can we say that this device of the reversed text is the same when, as with Perelman, the mirrored poems are separated by only one page within the same sequence, yet in Bernstein's case do not even appear within the same book?

The answer to these questions is to be found in how we conceive of the part: whole relations of the poem. Each device is determined by its relationship to the whole. This might be called the first axiom of the poetic device, to which we must now add a second, based on the implications of the privilege given to expectation, to the process of experiencing, in the generation of semantic shifts at all levels: *there is no such thing as a whole.* This is because time divides the poem: it can never, even on completion, be experienced "at once." The reader is always *at some point* with regard to the reading. This placement organizes the interpretation of details, including any ambiguities, but only temporarily. The perceptibility of a device, in fact, depends upon the reader's recognition of the process of reorganization itself.

In collapsing the poem to the privilege of the static text, New Critics and other advocates of an incomplete formalism lost sight not merely of the contributing participation of any a reader's experience, but also the dimension of an everpresent and *never stable* temporality. It is only in the light of a triangularity of these three dimensions—text, time, reader's experience—, that we can begin to ask, let along answer, the question: is coherence only an effect?

By coherence I do not simply intend to indicate *referentiality* as poets have come to use that word. Lyn Hejinian's *My Life*[29] is as powerful an argument for coherence as can be imagined, yet the text resolutely problematizes narrative constructions. The deliberate artificiality of its repeated phrases (true captions) is a necessary component in the book's vision of the constructedness of meaning per se. So that even if few of the sentences "follow" one another, a total envisionment of a unified presence is carried forward to the nth *degree*.

A sharp contrast to *My Life* is Kit Robinson's "A Sentimental Journey." Here is a fraction of the text:

Objectless abject.

Rode high for a week and on the seventh day I crashed.

Some of the more repulsive developments in avant garde music are waiting for you in bed. Women check a form of address leering from a window.

Worn out, I died, then hurried on.[30]

"A Sentimental Journey" proposes no totalizing envisionment, at least nothing more narrowly determined than *personality* or *writing*. Its variable short paragraphs argue against any unification as form or shape. Envisionments do occur, even built up between sentences, and may hold or reappear across several paragraphs. But none is dominant. There is no pointing away from some degree of the particular toward a whole, a whole which must always be *in some other place*. If there is any moment even nostalgic for closure, it occurs nine paragraphs before the end:

I've gone off on a tangent, but everything that organizes an individual is external to him. He's only the point where lines of force intersect.[31]

Robinson's work is not alone in its hostility or disinterest in any dream of totalization, but to the extent that it is more antagonistic to a unifying myth, like "person" or "the organic," than, say, Robert Creeley's *Pieces*, it is an oasis in what Max Jacob once rightly termed "the desert of art."

If, as "A Sentimental Journey" argues, coherence is just an effect, the first task in elaborating a new rhetoric of poetic devices currently in use would be to identify those which motivate the semantic shift of closure. The tyrannical privilege of totality and those devices which can be utilized to counter this "unity effect" need also to be explained. From this point, a shared vocabulary would be better able to assist poets and readers in the production and consumption of texts, to know, if not what the writer "is talking about," at least what is going on.

III ~~~~~~

Z-SITED PATH

I

Louis Zukofsky

The first (and for a long time the only) poet to read Pound and Williams with what we would recognize as a modern eye and ear. The ear tuned tautly toward a double function: *intrinsic*, language as he found it (i.e., parole); *extrinsic*, musical composition, determining wholeness, aesthetic consistency, perfect rest. But for whom language began with sight (thus *Bottom*—love : reason : eye : mind—in which love contains all the significations Walter Benjamin, so like Zukofsky, gave the term *aura*). In his writing, language (L) systhesizes polar impulses rising dialectically from an equally problematic material base:

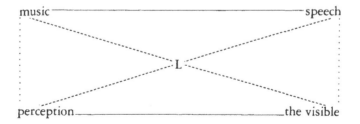

Not the Yiddish his parents spoke, Zukofsky's English always carries some trace of Other (hence *Catullus*), tending toward objectification. Each line and/or stanza is a study in balance, silence (peace) proposed as maximum stress in all directions, thus active.

This never-to-be-resolved equilibrium of the spoken within the written within the spoken, etc., is for Zukofsky the motivating center of craft (the final 28 lines of *"A"-23*, the actual last words in that composition, escort the reader through the alphabet: letters are presences).

"A living calendar . . . : music, thought, drama, story, poem." A characteristic distinction: the title is *"A"*, not *A*. Its open-ended interconnectedness in sections 1 through 6 marks a debt to *The Cantos*, but from 7 (with which he chose to represent himself in the Objectivist issue of *Poetry* in February, 1931) forward, a new conceptualization as to the function of part-to-whole relations in the formation of a longpoem begins to emerge: each section is a totalization, complete in itself, capable of entering into larger structures as an autonomous fact. This integrity of units is radically unlike, say, *The Maximus Poems* or Robert Duncan's "Passages," although it includes, indeed requires, the capacity to incorporate a piece in open form (*"A"- 12* his *Paterson*). This recognition that the sections of a large work must operate as a group, not as a series, empowers Zukofsky, in a sharp contrast to Pound, Williams or Olson, to complete or, more accurately, close the poem.

April 5, 1928: St. Matthew's Passion is performed at Carnegie Hall and Connie Mack's Philadelphia Athletics, about to embark on a new season of baseball, introduce a new uniform, abandoning their old elephant logo for a large letter *A*. These events are reported on facing pages in the Friday *New York Times*.

II

Influence, or Dr. Williams

Influence, that mediation which occurs during the composition of a text through its author's awareness of other writers and writings, is a process so particular to the individuals and works in question, that it is impossible to discuss in any but the most crudely reductive terms. Yet its impact on poetry, particularly in this century, would seem to be pervasive. It is the active element in the political transformation of writing into Literature.

David Gitin tells the story of how, when Robert Creeley first moved to Buffalo, all the local poets there began to write in shorter lines. Similarly, there was a period when it seemed that the younger poets in and around the "New York School" could be grouped according to whether their work bore the characteristic features of the poems of John Ashbery or those of Ted Berrigan. One person might find Ezra Pound's sense of history-as-theme to be crucial to their own idea of what writing legitimately should be. Other have focused on his conception of archival research as "what a writer does," or on his appropriation of collage technique from the visual arts. Still others have found his rigorous exploration of metrics, or the role of translation as a self-conscious learning process for a poet, to be the most useful aspect of his work. There are those for whom the early poems are the epitome of Pound's practice, with *The Cantos* being integral to a disintegration that led, finally, to his long-term psychiatric hospitalization. There are others who find *The Cantos* to represent a dramatic step into the 20th century, an evolution toward a writing shaped as much by the present realities of the world *as form* as by any inherited sense of traditional modes, a sharp contrast from the crabbed, closed poetry of much of his earlier work. And there are even those, more than a few, who come to Pound for his anti-Semitism and crank economics. There's a parable about blind men and an elephant that suggests what it means to be Poundian in 1985.

As a process, influence is active and seldom neutral. The three ghosts that hover visibly over the texts of Richard Brautigan are Lew Welch, a suicide, Ernest Hemingway, a suicide, and Jack Spicer, who killed himself through alcohol abuse at the age of 41. In writing as in life, the examples set by elders and peers can function as possibilities, suggestions of directions that remain to be fully explored. Yet for some poets they serve instead as limits, the outer reaches beyond which poetry may not travel. The widespread howling and derision which has greeted the tendency which has come to be characterized as "language poetry" reflects precisely this taboo against transcending the known universe. In this sense, the collective influence of generations of writers functions as a cultural (psychological *and* ideological) screen: the outcries of those poets and critics for whom the arrival of anything new in the field of writing is, literally, impossible is an index of just how painful the recognition of one's own cultural borders can be.

Just as literature is the social organization of writing, the transformation of all texts into a shaped (and highly edited) canon, there can be no telling of literary history which does not, however implicitly, contain a theory of periodization: the grouping together in time of a cohesive ensemble of tendencies. Literature could as easily be depicted synchronically as a spatial field composed of "movements" or clusters of writers sharing important characteristics. In either case, such representation depicts a foreground constituted precisely by the suppression of "extraneous" detail (which can include entire groups of writers). Nothing demonstrates the power of this process—which, to reiterate, is at once both psychological and ideological—more clearly than the universalization of the influence of William Carlos Williams.

No poet in the 20th century has come to be seen as more "All American" than this Rutherford pediatrician, a phenomenon that may obscure, ironically, recognition of his Puerto Rican heritage, and which may be reducible (if the somewhat similar aspect of the public images of both Allen Ginsberg and Bruce Springsteen are any indication) to an identification of the stereotypical national experience with the culture found in the smaller cities and towns of New Jersey. Williams' verse is also taken to be the apotheosis of clarity, the "unmarked voice" against which every other poet's work can be compared for its stylization and artifice. In a variety of capacities, his writing has been an active force within poetry for 60 years. While he has by no means been alone in shaping American writing since the Second World War, Williams is a particularly instructive case, not merely because of the central role his poems played in making possible the literary revolution of the 1950s, but also because his presence made inevitable the eventual popular rediscovery of a number of other authors, particularly the Objectivists, whose reintroduction into the foreground of the canon in the 60s not only gave form to much of that decade's writing, but also forced a re-examination of Williams' work in the light of their own, the result of which has been a multiplication of possible readings and a diaspora of impacts, to the extent that the question "Do you read Williams?", so fundamental to the fifties, can be replaced now with "Which is the Williams you think you read?" For every poet who has felt the impact of Pound's innovations, there are a score who operate under the far-more-readable spell of Williams. That virtually every American poet can now be called "Williamsesque" has rendered the term meaningless.

When I was an undergraduate at San Francisco State and Berkeley in the late sixties, there was an assumption on both campuses that the revolution, in literature at least, had been successful. It was commonplace by then for instructors to send students to certain works of Williams (and it was *not* mentioned that such pieces represented only a fraction of his total output or concerns) as exemplars of clarity in verse-statement and of the strict subordination of form to function:

As the cat
climbed over
the top of

the jamcloset
first the right
forefoot

carefully
then the hind
stepped down

into the pit of
the empty
flowerpot[1]

This poem, older than its readers, was to be the gesture of the utterly contemporary! With its *jamcloset* designating an object few, if any, of us had ever seen. With its false parallel between *right* and *hind*. With its two run-on words, a stylistic flourish that places its author squarely in the generation of Faulkner and Joyce. With its equation of line length to the physical movement of the cat, a device so deliberately cute as to be cloying.

Often poems such as this were accompanied with some background information suggesting that prior to 1950 Williams had been considered marginal and obscure. Yet, as Paul Mariani's biography demonstrates, this was not the case, but more likely reflected a partisan requirement that for the literary revolt of the New American poets to have been a success there needed to be a previous condition of sufficient oppression. While there was indeed a situation of neglect for the bulk of the Objectivists, Williams suffered little. Why Williams should have been considered obscure was never evident and the issue, if pressed, merely led to the response that the New Critics and the academic poets they cultivated had different literary values. Yet, as Josephine Miles once told David Melnick and myself, writers of her generation "didn't know how to read him." So, apparently a chasm *had* been opened and been crossed. What once had been opaque was now the essence of lucidity. Looking backward with an educated and biased eye, it was impossible to do more than wonder at the nature of the cataclysm. That conservative poetry which, we were told, had once cast Williams into the shadows now seemed linguistically dead and spiritually pointless. In the minds of many undergraduates, the "Establishment" in poetry, which surrounded writers like Robert Lowell and Richard Wilbur, was one with the same establishment which was attempting to prosecute an imperialist war in Indochina. Robert McNamara even sat on the board of the foundation which published the magazine *Poetry*.

There is of course a critical element of oppositionality in the work of William Carlos Williams, as indeed there is in Stein, Zukofsky, Olson or Creeley. In each instance it lies in the identification of method with content. Opposition to the horrors of daily life in the twentieth century, whether or not these are equated with any given social and economic system, is expressed through opposition to the normative or inherited practices of that literature which embodies the status quo. One need only read *Spring & All, The Mayan Letters* or *Proprioception* to see that this writing presumes that perception itself is not possible within the confines of cultural norms. Poetry, according to Williams, is defined as "new form dealt with as a reality in itself," or, again, "the perfection of new forms as additions to nature." Even in the distorted version offered by Pound, it is evident that this "poetics of the new" represents a fundamentally utopian project.

In the schools on the west coast at least, the step beyond Williams meant *The New American Poetry*, Donald Allen's 1960 gathering of 44 poets, including Ashbery, Paul Blackburn, Gregory Corso, Creeley, Ed Dorn, Duncan, Larry Eigner, Ginsberg, Le Roi Jones, Jack Kerouac, Kenneth Koch, Denise Levertov, Michael McClure, Frank O'Hara, Olson, Gary Snyder, Spicer, Welch, Philip Whalen and John Wieners. These younger writers had, it seemed, taken up the path Williams and old friend Pound has so bravely forged.

History reorganizes the past through just such reductions.

Williams and often Pound had been pictured either as loners working in an essential isolation or as extensions of something which, long ago in an almost mythic past, had gone by the name of Imagism and meant also the likes of Richard Aldington, H.D. and Marianne Moore. Somehow—and the vagueness here should have given it away—Olson had seen fit to make of "Projective Verse" a declaration of poetics as practiced by Williams at a moment (1950) when the doctor's literary marginality should have made that seem the unlikeliest of projects. What, in retrospect, made Olson's pronouncement revolutionary was in good part only the failure of educators (and publishers) to admit the complexities, and sustain the continuities, of actual practice. Olson was only six years younger than Zukofsky, two younger than George Oppen. Duncan had been reading Zukofsky since the thirties.

The defining issue which seemed to confront young, would-be "new" poets at the moment the Allen anthology made the work of the fifties available on a national scale was one of traditions, camps. According to Allen's own summation of the "New American" faction, "it has shown one common characteristic: a total rejection of all those qualities typical of academic verse." In 1965, the Paris Leary/Robert Kelly anthology, *A Controversy of Poets*, attempted to address this either/or structure directly, presenting "both sides." Even as late as 1973, David Antin, whose "talking pieces" are closed forms every bit as conventionalized as any sonnet, felt it meaningful to say, as he did at San Francisco State that "if robert lowell *(sic)* is a poet i dont want to be a poet."

Historically, the most important aspect of this dispute was the presumption of a centralized legitimation for poetry, of a homogenous reading public to be fought over and won. The reality was, and is, that Antin and Lowell came from, and spoke to, different communities. To deny either writer the status of poet is not so much to question their skill or vision as it is to deny the readers of each the legitimacy of their own existence *as a community*. It is in this sense that Jerome Rothenberg rightly, if hyperbolically, compares such consciously exclusionary canon-formation as that of Harold Bloom's with the practices of Dr. Josef Mengele at Auschwitz. Whether carried out under the guise of criticism or as a contest of bards, what is hidden is the fact of the struggle between different groups (not, in this instance, necessarily classes) within the larger social ensemble of the nation. The question is not, as Bloom formulates it, "Which poet shall live?" but which community shall dominate the other, whose set of values will prevail.

The history of poetry since the Allen anthology has been one of decentralization, of the destruction of this founding false binary premise. The causes, both within and without the terrain of literature, are many and complex. The civil rights and student movements of the 60s, the resistance to the war in Indochina, and the self-destruction of the Nixon administration all substantially altered America's collective self-image. The long economic expansion, which began at the close of the Second World War only to end abruptly with the oil embargo of 1974, transformed the nature of work (and worker) in the U.S., and made possible the vast expansion of postsecondary education to new sectors of the society, an expansion which saw many of the New American poets incorporated into the very academy they had proposed themselves as the alternative to. The rise of a "middle-strata" or "new Petty Bourgeoisie" or "Yuppie" culture, of a powerful and still-growing feminist movement, and of an "oppositional culture" in general cannot be dissociated from these circumstances. Poetry was destined to change no matter which side won the "revolt" of the 50s, not merely because the content of daily life had changed, but also because the makeup of possible audiences was no longer the same.

The so-called low-cost technology of the "small press revolution" was not the creator of this transformation in poetry, simply the mechanism through which it was carried out. While its contribution to the democratization of the resources of production has sometimes been overstated, its decentralizing (if not anarchic) impact on distribution has been almost as profound.

Further, both "sides" were undergoing extensive reorganization. By 1971, among the New Americans alone, O'Hara, Spicer, Kerouac, Blackburn and Olson were dead. Others, including Dorn, Levertov, Amiri Baraka (Jones) and Ashbery, were to substantially change their own writing—and their audiences. Of the formulations posed by the Allen anthology, only the New York School remained loosely intact, and with Berrigan's arrival it too had begun to imply different values and include different people. In addition, tendencies not foreseen by the Allen book, such as the work of Antin, Rothenberg or Jackson Mac Low, complicate matters. And

Rothenberg's anthologies, a sustained assault on the racist notion of literature as a European-centered art form, deepened the critique of a homogenous writing with "timeless" values, while foregrounding (in a way that could not have been done prior to the Vietnam War) the problematic nationalism many of the New Americans seemed to derive from Williams.

But the single most significant change in American poetry is to be found in the central role of writing within feminist culture, which by 1985 is (for good reason) the largest of all existing verse audiences. By taking control of their own aesthetic destiny, the women of this movement, itself an ensemble of social formations, have shifted the entire center of debate away from the academic versus New American, or any other simple dichotomy. In so doing, they have ensured the decentralization—and contextualization—of American poetry.

Thus, even if the poetic revolution was a momentary success, its fruits were remarkably problematic. The New American poets had articulated, as had Pound, Williams, Stein and many of the other high modernists, a literature centered not in the institutionalized social environment of college campuses, but in the cities (and linked to oppositional cultural movements). Yet many of the poets of the Allen anthology had been incorporated into an expansionary educational system where they co-existed more or less uneasily with the competing poetics of other faculty members. Out of this a new generation of younger writers (and critics) was beginning to emerge, often trained *professionally* by this movement of iconoclasts (although, without exception, always also by more conservative writers and teachers as well), and were themselves moving rapidly into positions as educators. Unlike their mentors, these younger poets were characterized precisely by their not having ever been apart from the American educational bureaucracy. Few, if any, of the writers in the Allen anthology appear to ever have been hired to teach on the grounds of their professional education as teachers. Yet few of the "protege" generation ever appear to have been hired because of their poetry. In many instances, these younger writer/teachers have further contributed to the decentralization of poetry by creating out of their patchwork influences a new poetics of the "middle-ground," a neo-academic verse in which the most pronounced literary influence is none other than William Carlos Williams. What remains are the surface features of Williams' poetry. What is profoundly absent is the identification of method with content, and any recognition of a linkage between this and a broader social vision. In dramatically extending the message of Williams over a period of three decades, what has been lost is the essential oppositionality of his work. What is missing is precisely its challenge to the perceptual limits of the reader. In a nation in which any literate individual can, unproblematically, read much of William Carlos Williams, that which has become truly opaque, even invisible, is the work of William Carlos Williams.

III

Third Phase Objectivism

Objectivism's third or renaissance period was marked by the resurrection of the works of Zukofsky, Oppen, Basil Bunting, Carl Rakosi, Charles Reznikoff and Lorine Niedecker to public attention virtually overnight in the early 1960s. This has proven the most problematic of that literary tendency's phases, simultaneously its most influential and least cohesive time, mixing a resurgence of interest in existing texts with the production of new writings. The definition of Objectivism was altered just as that curious rubric was, in turn, being used to rewrite the literary history of the thirties and forties. Objectivism's absence, the long second phase of neglect, was attributable, at least in part, to the fact that these poets had not created a sufficient network of support, particularly lacking a magazine, before many of them turned their attention elsewhere during the years of the depression and World War II—and, not coincidentally, because several were Marxists and Jews. Their long "silence" contributed significantly to the extremism of form and content which so many of the New American poets had found necessary to bridge the distance between themselves and those twin sources of a rigorous, open-form, speech-based poetics, Pound and Williams. Not surprisingly, the return of the Objectivists was to coincide with a tempering and toning down of just this extremism, and the formation of not so much a neo-objectivist movement as a "middle road" halfway between the New Americans and those

136

academics who'd moved on their own toward a poetry founded on speech, both in open form and syllabics. This middle road, which was first to reach the public through the *San Francisco Review*, the third series of *Origin, Poetry* during the last seven years of Henry Rago's editorship, and later through a series of tightly-edited little magazines, including *Maps, Ironwood, Occurrence, Paper Air* and *Montemora*, has substantially altered the contours of American verse, although it has received relatively little attention as a phenomenon in its own right.

That the revival period of the Objectivists would prove less cohesive could have been expected. Men and women in their sixties, their aesthetics and work fully formed (and, in some instances, largely behind them), have fewer needs for peer group response than do writers in their twenties. Nor, unlike first phase Objectivism, did they now have to rely on one another for publication and the other support services which normally characterize any collective literary activity.

The actual products of Objectivism's final period are not many, but they are significant: Bunting's addition of *Briggflats* to an essentially completed *oeuvre;* Zukofsky's return for only the second time in twenty years (there had been a period of work between 1948 and 1951) to the poem *"A"*, composing 11 new sections and adding his wife Celia's *L.Z. Masque* to finish the project; Rakosi's return as a writer of short, witty, lyrical poems; and 95% of the works of George Oppen. It is this last fact, the "return" of Oppen from decades of silence to a place *beyond* that which he had taken during the earlier periods, which fundamentally defines third phase Objectivism, transforming it from the aesthetically radical and oppositional poetry of the early thirties to a more conservative (aesthetically, if not politically) phenomenon which then served as the foundation for the ensuing middle road. This transformation is registered most clearly in the recent *Chicago Review* feature on Objectivism, which is incoherent from the perspective of the first phase, but consistent with this much later version.

There is more to this evolution than the mere addition of new poems gaining one writer greater weight within a collective whole. Oppen's works, from *The Materials* onward, are decisively different than *Discrete Series*, his first phase volume. This shift is precisely one of stance, and it may well be that a quarter century of struggle, with the constraints of daily life, marriage, parenting, with war and exile, with capitalism and its Frankenstein, fascism, render the later position inevitable. However, it is not difficult to demonstrate that it falls outside the original, loosely-held program of phase one Objectivism. It is only necessary to contrast the later work with a piece such as the review of *Discrete Series* written by Williams for *Poetry* under the title of "The New Poetical Economy," which reads in part:

> The appearance of a book of poems, if it be a book of good poems, is an important event because of relationships the work it contains will have with thought and accomplishment in other contemporary reaches of the intelligence. This leads to a definition of the term "good." If the poems in the book constitute necessary corrections of or emendations to human conduct in their day, both as to thought and manner, then they are good. But if these changes originated in the poems, causing thereby a direct liberation of the intelligence, then the book becomes of importance to the highest degree.
>
> But this importance cannot be in what the poem says, since in that case the fact that it is a poem would be a redundancy. The importance lies in what the poem *is*. Its existence as a poem is of first importance, a technical matter, as with all facts, compelling the recognition of a mechanical structure. A poem which does not arouse respect for the technical requirements of its own mechanics may have anything you please painted all over it or on it in the way of meaning but it will for all that be as empty as a man made of wax or straw.
>
> It is the acceptable fact of a poem as a mechanism that is the proof of its meaning and this is as technical a matter as in the case of any other machine. Without the poem being a workable mechanism in its own right, a mechanism which arises from, while at the same time it constitutes the meaning of, the poem as a whole, it will remain ineffective. And what it says regarding the use or worth of that particular piece of "propoganda" which it is detailing will never be convincing.[2]

Beginning with *The Materials*, Oppen, contrary to the admonitions of this highly partisan piece of writing, demonstrated himself to be a master in calling attention to *the importance in what the poem says*. This he achieved through a variety of devices. The sheer number of the techniques he employed make it evident that this new conceptualization of meaning was, in fact, a difference in

138

position and not (as rigid adherence to the tenets of phase one Objectivism might lead one to conclude) a decay in skills brought about by decades of disuse:

(1) a formal rhetorical tone, sometimes utilizing inversions of syntax or the parallel construction of examples, each punctuated with an *and*, implying sobriety of context;

(2) the use of adjectives which, value-laden, impart as much of *judgement* as they do of description;

(3) the use of repetition, which in Oppen's work ne ·ly always carries the tone away from that of speech, positing a su¡ 'e¡ent of emotion beyond the content of the repeated term itself;

(4) the use of spacing and silence to cast certain terms and phrases into a highly defined frame;

(5) the placement of key terms at critical locales on the line itself (no one in Oppen's generation was so sensitive to the fact that placement itself alters semantics, that the last word in a line carries the greatest weight, but that the first word carries the next most, so that any line beginning *and* and *of* carries a formality beyond that of the words themselves); and

(6) the use of plurals or mass nouns, rather than particulars or individuals, as objects for description and discussion.

Several of these mechanisms can be observed together in the two stanza fourth section of the sequence "Tourist Eye":

The heart pounds
To be among them, the buildings,
The red buildings of Red Hook! In the currents of the harbor
The barn-red ferries on their curving courses
And the tides of Buttermilk Channel
Flow past the Brooklyn Hardware stores

And the homes
The aging homes
Of the workmen. This is a sense of order
And of threat. The essential city,
The necessary city
Among these harbor streets still visible.[3]

They are even more visible in the later poem "Exodus":

> Miracle of the children   the brilliant
> Children   the word
> Liquid as woodlands   Children?
>
> When she was a child I read Exodus
> To my daughter   "the children of Israel . . . "
>
> Pillar of fire
> Pillar of cloud
>
> We stared at the end
> Into each other's eyes   Where
> She said hushed
>
> Were the adults   We dreamed to each other
> Miracle of the children
> The brilliant children   Miracle
>
> Of their brilliance   Miracle
> of[4]

Note that final lower case *o*.

It is not as if no other Objectivist poet employed such techniques, even to the same ends. Consider *"A"- 10*, for example. Yet none went so far as to make them the grounds for an entire poetics, which Oppen did. One can imagine that the response of the partisan Williams of the thirties to this stance would not be positive. "Who," for instance, is the first of the two voices in the 38th section of *Of Being Numerous*, a character created wholly out of the placement of the word *last*, the rhetorical closure of the statements via the repeated terms *You* and *Nurse,* and the increased formality gained by the final use of the word *him* in the third stanza?

> You are the last
> Who will know him
> Nurse.

Not know him,
He is an old man,
A patient,
How could one know him?

You are the last
Who will see him
Or touch him,
Nurse.[5]

But one must remember that Williams was a partisan to a particular cause, that there was the academic tradition in American poetry which was then much more prevalent and substantial, in terms of publications and critical support (and jobs) than anything he, Pound and these young followers had going for them. There was, in short, a battle being waged which had largely been settled, if not forgotten, by the time *The Materials* appeared, a year before Williams' death. (This should not be confused with the one then being conducted by the New American poets, although this latter confrontation was, in a sense, a direct historic descendant, and the momentary success of their revolt provided the context in which the Objectivists as a whole re-emerged.) The problem which confronted George Oppen in the early 60s was not one of either/or, but rather the possibility of demonstrating to that alternate, conservative tendency in poetry *how it might be done better by other principles*, specifically Objectivist in origin.

So it is not surprising that Oppen should be the bridge-poet between the tendency known as the New American poetry and those of the middle-ground, an accomplishment of third phase Objectivism which helped to restructure the entire field of American verse.

IV

Why the MLA Can't Read

Barry Ahearn's *Zukofsky's "A": An Introduction*[6] presents the first booklength attempt to come to terms with this 800 page work. Ahearn's subtitle is literal. The book is ideally suited as an aid to those potential readers who have been put off by the notorious alleged difficulty and/or very real linguistic density of Zukofsky's text. It is not, we are cautioned, "a guide to the poem: no one knows enough . . . to write one. It is rather a history of the poem's growth." With that, Ahearn presents a brief sketch of the poet's youth, notes the relation of *"A"* to the earlier "Poem Beginning 'The'" and launches into a reading of the larger work, following the chronology of its composition rather than the numbering of its 24 sections.

The chronological approach diverts, if not defuses, the question of difficulty by "humanizing" the work. It also enables Ahearn to approach the poem as autobiography, a major and problematic concern. No other practitioner of the American longpoem has so thoroughly located the events of her or his telling in the actions and structures of the poet's own daily life. Yet the process of composition has so transformed these referents into textuality that an opaque music of hollowed-out signifiers is often felt to be the result. How many ardent readers of this most "family-centered" of poems are aware, for example, that fully one-third of it was written while Zukofsky was still a bachelor? Much of Ahearn's gloss consists precisely in providing personal detail rather than analysis. The dead Ricky of *"A"* - *3* turns out to be the younger brother of Whittaker Chambers, Zukofsky's college friend and erstwhile Objectivist poet who later became the top editor of *Time* and a key figure in the McCarthy era. The punned Arbutus of the final line of the 23rd movement—"z-sited path are but us"—is the name of the street on which Louis' son Paul then lived. Such bits of information do indeed expand the ground of signification from which a reader can enter into the play of the poem. And to present this data in the sequence of arrangement, rather than composition, would be to subject the reader to a baffling series of flash-forwards and flashbacks.

Which, however, would seem to be what Zukofsky intended.

This is the problem which confronts Ahearn's strategy, one

which, even as Ahearn himself points to it dozens of times, eludes *Zukofsky's "A"*. It is not the purpose of that poem to make of itself a "whole." Not at least in the traditional sense of a hierarchical and referential structure which would carry the reader's attention away from what was actually right there on the page, toward some (always deferred) moment of total "unification." Unity in *"A"* is constituted first at the level of musical (formal) organization. The primary function of a given statement is not its contribution toward a thematic association or image, even while it is "perfectly clear," so much as in its contextualization within the present language of a particular usage. In a 1935 letter to Lorine Niedecker cited by Ahearn, Zukofsky writes:

> it must be music of the statements, but not explanation ever, that's why I seem to leave out—but the reader will have to learn to read statement, juxtaposed constructs, as music.[7]

In an earlier essay on Apollinaire, Zukofsky characterizes the French poet's work as "composition as action." Ahearn quotes the passage, seeing in it an example of how, for Zukofsky, "Distinctions between the artist and what he *(sic)* produces (or consumes) grow fuzzier and fuzzier." But, if the reader begins from the perspective of formal (musical) organization, that is, if the reader were to give to the word "action" essentially the same meaning it would possess for painters such as Jackson Pollack (and Zukofsky is specifically discussing the impact of painting on Apollinaire), then quite the opposite conclusion must be drawn: the poem is a complex signifier, the poet is not. A poet's life is a signified. A complex signifier, if it is to possess a meaning, must manifest itself according to a strict temporal sequence. Temporal, as in music. That Zukofsky should give primacy to the signifier as the dominant feature of language should come as no surprise. It is this principle which justifies his phonetic "translations" from the Hebrew in the 15th section, of *Rudens* in the 21st, and elsewhere from Catallus. If any further evidence needs to be mustered as to the poem's reliance on formal organization as the dynamic through which the unity of *"A"* must come into being, we need look only to what Ahearn calls "ur-plan" for the piece on a scrap of paper in the Zukofsky Collection at the University of Texas. This "earliest sketch" is not the declaration of an autobiography yet to be lived, but the mapping out of a structure: a poem to be composed in 24 parts.

Ahearn is not unaware of the difficulties posed by his approach. Nor unamused. In fact, a good part of the pleasure to be found in his book lies in watching a superb debater argue a position he knows to be untenable. If, from the 19th movement on, "the poem looks increasingly like an experiment in English as a foreign language," it's because English *is* a foreign language, a motley of other tongues imposed from the outside upon any individual. Ahearn goes so far as to concede the case entirely:

> All criticism attempts to match its own terms with the work in question. If one of the tests of value is the degree to which the work resists such attempts, *"A"* passes with flying colors.[8]

Yet, only four pages further (and just two from the end), he appears to apprehend the central dominance which the continuous present of musical (temporal) organization holds over thematic or referential abstractions: "By now it should be apparent that the nooks and crannies of the poem are the places where its essence resides."[9] This, this, this, this.

The larger problem here is that criticism, not Ahearn, is still unready and unable to read a poem begun over 55 years ago. Criticism as an industry. As opposed to thought. The ultimate demand to seek a predominantly thematic or referential unity, the first order of all Anglo-American criticism, capsizes in the face of a work such as *"A"*. It is to Ahearn's credit that he admits this.

But is that enough? The very project of coming to this conclusion is one of asking certain questions while leaving other, far more important ones unasked. Ahearn's entire critique of the 16th movement is that it "hardly seems serious."[10] Yet the entire proposition of a 4 word poem as 1/24th of an 800 page work invokes a host of problems of form, scale and integrity which could easily be the basis for a book the size of Ahearn's. Similarly dismissed is the 10th section, which "shows the strain [of World War II] on its author; it is much less ambitious than its companion movements."[11] No mention is made of the degree to which this war poem derives from the work of, and forms an homage to, Apollinaire, killed in the previous war. (One example: the broken cafe chatter of "Lundi rue Christine" becomes the interrupted telecommunications with Paris.) "Putting aside the issues raised by the 'Iyyob' passage (they are legion)," Ahearn never returns to them—even though the physical presentness of these "translated" Hebraic phonemes is an instance of Zukofsky's insistence on *presence*, the central thesis of his *Bottom*—which Ahearn, *quoting Zukofsky verbatim*, dismisses as "500 pages about Shakespeare just to say one thing, the natural human eye is OK, but it's that erring brain that's no good, and he says it all the time."[12] Given this stance, it is not surprising that the one major text by Zukofsky that is never mentioned by Ahearn is *Catallus*, Zukofsky's most musical and "non-referential" work.

At its best, Ahearn's approach combines an infusion of personal detail with an inspection of Zukofsky's editing of his own source material, most usefully Veblen. At its worst, it falls into psychological speculation. Having pinned his dislike on *"A"-10* on the influence of the war, after which Zukofsky did not begin another section for 8 years, Ahearn writes of "the despair that silenced him during those years," ignoring the completion of *A Test of Poetry*, the composition of large portions of *Prepositions, It Was*, and *Ferdinand*, over 40 short poems, the revision of the first six sections of *"A"*, and the start on *Bottom*. No reason at all is offered for the longer "silence" between 1951 and 1960.

This over-reaching for thematic, autobiographical or psychological unity shows up at other levels. Although the first half of the 9th movement was the only work of Zukofsky's to receive an exegesis by its author—a 41 page citation of sources and comparative translations—, Ahearn largely relegates this self-critique to an appendix and fails to test his own approach to the poem against it. Yet his own is visibly at odds with the text here:

> The second half of *"A" - 9 (sic)* exists as a preindustrial scene, reversing the setting of the first half (which was apparently a factory or warehouse).[13]

At the end of the *First Half of "A"- 9*, Zukofsky actually "restates" in prose the content of every stanza. If the text of the poem itself were not clear enough to make evident that the only "place" or "scene" which is set for either half is in the words of the poem itself (the poem is a "place"), then the restatement of Zukofsky's Coda certainly should be:

Applied mathematics employs a quantity called "Action" defined as the product of energy and time. Perhaps things are such quanta of "Action" when they are defined as time congealed labor. But now the poem first brought into being by this abstract evaluation has been forced to turn from it to the labor present in the words of the song itself, the form of which the things speaking have assumed.[14]

By its generous reading of the work *and* its inability to come to any terms with it, Ahearn's *Zukofsky's "A"* shows the great power of the poem to insist on its own autonomy, especially in the face of criticism's demand for referential or thematic "unity." It gives a glimpse of what institutional academic thought is going to have to transcend if it is again to make any claim to literacy. Zukofsky is of course but one of any number of possible examples of this problem. From Gertrude Stein to the present, poets have increasingly emphasized that meaning in poetry falls on the side of the signifier—and that it is not deferred to any hierarchic abstraction such as character, plot or argument. It is only through the signifier that the cultural limits of the self, the subject, become visible. It is there, and there only, that direct perception takes place in a poem. This above all else is what still separates the tradition of poets who move into the new from the rest. More than any other critical text I can think of, Ahearn's book demonstrates just how the hidden agendas of academic training, bureaucratizing meaning into a fetish of the signified, rob intelligent people of the ability to read.

SPICER'S LANGUAGE

Twenty years after his death, the poetry of Jack Spicer seems to have survived quite well. His writing is more widely and sympathetically read today than ever before. But not necessarily more wisely. There remains around Spicer's work an aura of mystery which serves to buffer a reader from further (or, at least, other) use of the work.

The reasons for this are many. While Spicer's insistence that he did not "like his life written down" is integral to his entire project as a poet, the effect of this is less one of focusing attention on the writing-as-such, than of inserting into the place of the writer's biography a narcissistic absence. This same absent presence also lies at the heart of the silence held by certain Eastern religious figures, such as Meher Baba, and is similarly inscribed within more Western and secular phenomena, such as baseball's Steve Carlton's refusal to talk to reporters or the Lone Ranger's mask. Always it is the absence which empowers the presence, a contradiction or overdetermination that yields (in the eyes of a believer or an engaged reader) a vision of absolute Other.

The degree to which Spicer intended such a figure of romance is unclear. Nonetheless, the position of an "invisible life" conspires with a series of external events to render such mythologizing inevitable. One was his public image as bar-hound and bad-boy of the postwar San Francisco poetry scene—in which he was a (if not *the*) central figure. Another was his death at the early age of 40. Soon after, his two final (and most mature) collections, *Language* and *Book of Magazine Verse*, were posthumously published, reinforcing the impression of an absent presence. After these went out of print, it was virtually impossible to find an authorized edition of a book by Jack Spicer for years, elevating (or reducing) his work to the status of myth.

This mythic model is surprisingly linear. The writing can be read as becoming increasingly more intense, book to book, poem to poem, until finally, in the tenth poem "for *Downbeat*," addressing Allen Ginsberg, it reiterates a final cry of despair, "People are starving," before vanishing altogether, part will-o-the-wisp, part burning bush, part Cheshire cat: poof. As if Spicer knew all along that it was his writing that was sucking him toward an inevitable destruction, an attraction he was unable to resist. According to this reading, Spicer is pulled knowingly into the maelstrom of language. "My vocabulary did this to me," Robin Blaser cites as his next-to-last words.

Death is a major figure in *Language*, but not in the later *Book of Magazine Verse*. This alone should alert a reader to be wary of any model of nihilistic intensification, for it directly contradicts the central (if unspoken) premise of that model. Spicer was not, to use the words of one of his Magic Workshop students, Jack Gilbert, a "helot to the baptist hegemony of death."

In fact, a major consequence of the superimposition of a mythic reading onto the work of Jack Spicer is to render two very different books, *Language* and *Magazine Verse*, into a sort of diptych. I want instead to propose a reading which accentuates their dissimilarities.

On the surface, these books share important features. Each is a unified work constructed from seven shorter series of poems, a model of the book as a closed form Spicer had been developing for at least eight years, and a virtual duplication of the structure of the immediately preceding *The Holy Grail*. Whereas each of the seven sections of *Grail* were composed of seven poems, an almost Baudelairean sense of structural symmetry, the sections in both *Language* and *Magazine Verse* vary considerably in the number of poems (from two to sixteen). The cover of the first edition of each volume suggests a parallel conception. The pale green cover of *Language* is in fact a representation of the linguistics journal of that name, altered with a large red scrawl indicating the name of the book of poems, author and publisher. The deep brown cover of *Magazine Verse* is a carefully executed parody of the cover of *Poetry*, the Chicago magazine which, edited by Henry Rago and still benefitting from its long relationship with Ezra Pound, exercised a far greater centralizing influence on American poetics in the early

60s than any journal does today.

But the seven part structure and imitation magazine covers are only surface features. The book *Language* has virtually nothing to do with the magazine, beyond the coincidence of Spicer having co-authored, in the issue whose cover is reproduced, an article entitled "Correlation methods of comparing idiolects in a transition area" (apparently the one professional publication of Spicer's career as an academic linguist). In sharp contrast, most, if not all, of the sections in *Magazine Verse* relate more or less directly to the publications they ostensibly were written "for." It is not simply that the governing figure of the poems for *The St. Louis Sporting News* is baseball, nor that theological questions dominate the poems for the then-Catholic academic quarterly, *Ramparts*—there is a further layering of references. In the third of the poems for *Poetry Chicago*, Spicer writes "In the far, fat Vietnamese jungles nothing grows;" many mid-60s readers could have been expected to recognize that line's sardonic contrast to "The greens of the Ganges delta exfoliate," the first line of the first of John Berryman's four "Dream Songs" which appeared in the 50th anniversary double issue of *Poetry*.

This level of reference in *Magazine Verse* to periodicals as dissimilar as *The Nation, Downbeat* and *Tish* is unlike the experience of the book *Language*, the concerns of which are so thoroughly intertwined from beginning to end that its sense of closure is claustrophic.

Consider the opening section, "Thing Language," the longest sequence in either book. This title demonstrates overdetermination: the failure (or refusal) of an idea or image to add up (or reduce down) to any single entity. *Overdetermination is the essential Spicerian effect.* No logos, it implies, can exist which does not contain contradiction, negation or some effacing otherness within itself. This relates to the concept of an absent presence, the notion that you can have your cake and have (always, already) eaten it too. Spicer achieves this effect by yolking together two nouns, e.g. *thing* and *language*, into an adjective:noun relation in which the range of connotations surrounding each fail to overlap. The result is not quite an oxymoron, which would be too simple. The use of the nominative *thing* in the place of an adjective is more in line with the abominations of Leviticus, that thing and language shall not lie down together. As a linguist would know, things are not signs. They

149

are not, in a linguistic sense, significant. Nor, conversely, are signs things. Signs have no *positive* reference; they mean, by themselves, nothing, but are defined solely by their differences within a larger total system. Yet both the universe of things and the system of language are "total" dimensions of reality. An inarticulate universe of all that is real versus a system of articulation which, as a whole, can communicate nothing. Language constitutes the subject, that "I" which speaks and can recognize experience, through a medium which irrevocably cleaves the individual from the real. This is a vision of language, of subjectivity, as total isolation.

The first poem in "Thing Language" builds on this:

This ocean, humiliating in its disguises
Tougher than anything.
No one listens to poetry. The ocean
Does not mean to be listened to. A drop
Or crash of water. It means
Nothing.
It
Is bread and butter
Pepper and salt. The death
That young men hope for. Aimlessly
It pounds the shore. White and aimless signals. No
One listens to poetry.[1]

I take it as no accident that the first word of the first poem in *Language* is "This." The assertion of presence is language's most fundamental claim on subjectivity, the self-presence of the perceiving subject. "This *ocean*," a term charged from usages in Spicer's other writings. In *Language* and *Magazine Verse*, ocean stands as a primary figure of the natural world, absolute (inhuman) *force*. In "For Harvey" in the 1958 sequence *Admonitions*, the ocean appears as a mid-line parenthetical break in what may be Spicer's sharpest assault on the indulgences of "Projective verse":

When you break a line nothing
Becomes better.
There is no new (unless you are humming
Old Uncle Tom's Cabin) there is no new
Measure.
You breathe the same and Rimbaud

Would never even look at you.
Break
Your poem
Like you would cut a grapefruit
Make
It go to sleep for you
And each line (There is no Pacific Ocean) And make each line
Cut itself. Like seaweed thrown
Against the pier.[2]

This denial of the presence of the Pacific, contradicted (beyond the borders of the parenthesis) by the water schema of seaweed and pier, and erupting "without cause" in the midst of another discourse, is one of the first full-fledged instances of Spicer's use of overdetermination.

"This ocean, *humiliating in its disguises.*" To whom, or what? And what disguises? Spicer again combines terms whose connotative frames do not overlap. "Humiliating in its disguises" could easily possess a commonplace, if pointedly emotional, content given the appropriate context, but that is deliberately withheld from the reader by "This ocean." Yet any sense of these phrases being jammed together from different sources, as in collage technique, is muted by the sexually neutral pronoun "its," consistent as that can be with an ocean.

"Tougher than anything" asserts absoluteness of force. While this may subtly reiterate the claim of presence in "This ocean," a more powerful function lies in its sheer extremism. Furthermore, "Tougher than anything" can be understood in a variety of ways, depending on whether the ultimate referent is Mount St. Helens, Krazy-glu or Bette Davis. Here, the physical force of a vast mass of water is heavily conditioned by the anthropomorphism which lurks in the earlier "humiliating in its disguises." It is not simply that the natural universe is powerful, it is also (and perhaps more importantly) mean.

"No one listens to poetry." The internal tensions within the first sentence, significant as they are, pale in comparison to those between sentences. Here, and throughout Spicer's work, as with the parenthetical "There is no Pacific Ocean" from "For Harvey," the disjunctive nature of this sudden leap thoroughly anticipates the essential feature of the "new sentence."

This is a substantially different use of disjunction, *of difference itself,* from the strategies and devices which American and British poetry developed during the modernist period, following (more or less consciously) the models of collage and montage from the visual arts. Consider, for example, the opening of Ezra Pound's 84th Canto:

8th October:
    Si tuit li dolh el plor
        Angold   νέθνηκε

tuit lo pro, tuit lo bes
        Angold   νέθνηκε

"an' doan you think he chop an' change all the time
stubborn az a mule, sah, stubborn as a MULE,
got th' eastern idea about money"
        Thus Senator Bankhead
"am sure I don't know what a man like you
  would find to *do* here"
        said Senator Borah
Thus the solons, in Washington,
on the executive, and on the country, a.d. 1939

ye spotted lambe
        that is both blacke and white
is yeven to us for the eyes' delight

and now Richardson, Roy Richardson,
        says he is different
will I mention his name?

and Demattia is checking out.
        White, Fazzio, Bedell, *benedicti*
Sarnone, two Washingtons (dark) J and M
        Bassier, Starcher, H. Crowder and
no soldier he although his name is Slaughter

this day October the whateverth   Mr. Coxie
aged 91 has mentioned bonds and their
                         interest
apparently as a basis of issue
and Mr Sinc Lewis has not
        and Bartók has left us

and Mr Beard in his admirable condensation
(Mr Chas. Beard) has given one line to the currency
at about page 426 "The Republic"
We will be about as popular as Mr John Adams
and less widely perused
and the he leopard lay on his back playing with straw
in sheer boredom,

      (Memoirs of the Roman zoo)
        in sheer boredom[3]

In these lines Pound shifts scene, at least with regard to time and place, on six occasions. He uses three languages, not to mention his attempt at a Southern dialect, and mixes together a range of themes and topics. Yet the overall result, the sum of all these disjunctive features, is remarkably seamless.

The reasons are many. In only one of the six instances does the shift occur within a stanza. Each scene is at least three lines long, establishing a sense of atmosphere and internal rhythm. More importantly, these units proceed thematically toward an overall unity which is not, in the end, questioned. It willingly submits to the "tyranny of the whole." Presented as two passages from a diary, we move from Pound's mourning of the death of Angold, to a memory of his prewar trip to Washington, a snatch of verse in archaic English, the departure of still more friends, this time from the prison camp at Pisa, a commentary on the failure of history to understand economics (at least as Pound imagines himself to understand it) leading to his own cynical conclusion as to the future use of his own writing, followed by the image of a caged panther, idle in the Roman zoo, playing, as is Pound, with straw.

The entire passage is essentially constructed into one prosody that is far more in-built than it at first might seem. Beyond using lines of similar length and meter, Pound suppresses a sense of the sentence as unit by eliminating all but one terminal punctuation mark, while using "and" to create the least disruptive flow possible from one topic or scene to the next. Seven different lines begin with "and," three of them at the boundary between two images or scenes. "Thus" starts two other lines. Finally, the entire passage is replete with the interrelated mechanisms of parallel construction, repetition and rhyme.

To shape meaning in a reader's experience, semantic shifts

must be perceptible. Collage technique uses disjunction, or, more accurately, the conjunction of dissimilars, in order to free the structuring of the poem from the traditional demands imposed by narrative and/or exposition. Pound alters time, place, language and ostensible contents, while minimizing the reader's perception of these differences by linking the sub-units of the piece with common elements at the level of sound, syntax and theme. If the gap between the first two sentences in the initial poem of "Thing Language" is not an example of collage technique, it is because Spicer's use of this disjunctive moment, and its components, differs radically from that employed by Pound.

Pound's device is, literally, based on montage: its major shifts are scenic. The effect is one of a fragmented surface, under which lies a continuous and seamless deep structure. Even though the passage represents a very depressed moment in the life of a defeated man, Pound's ultimate position is clear: underneath, it all coheres. But in Spicer's piece, coherence and cohesion lie at the surface, masking-while-revealing a deeper chaos below.

Spicer's poem is composed in one stanza, written in what are ostensibly sentences, with a surface conventionality that extends to the capitalization of the letters at the lefthand margin. We have already seen the amount of tension which is set up in the first line by the irreducibility of the subject and its modifying clause to any single, simple envisionment. The leap to the second sentence is made *before a verb occurs in the first.* In being suppressed, this verb ("is"?) becomes yet another moment of an absent presence. And there are no less than five positions in the sentence which it could have taken, so that its absence (i.e., its presence) is not perceived at a single point, but instead floats freely, a syntactic equivalent of anxiety. Far more jolting to the reader, however, is that the two sentences, to a degree that is nowhere possible in the Pound passage, appear to come *from entirely different discourses.*

There are two or perhaps three ways to take the second sentence in the light of the first. One is to read it as an intensely emotional association, founded on the powerlessness of the individual poem contrasted against the vast pure force of nature. The second is to read it as a metacomment on the actual process we, the reader, are engaged in, reminding us in a somewhat Brechtian fashion that we are in fact in front of a poem, a machine made of words, and not "This ocean." Should this second reading be accepted, poetry and not the ocean becomes the subject of the piece. The very absoluteness of the assertion "No one listens to poetry" can be argued to reinforce either interpretation. The negative declaration can be viewed as the element which insinuates emotion *per se* into the association and contrast. Or it can be viewed as necessary to shock the reader out of the referential illusion of presence, "This ocean."

A third conceivable interpretation can be constructed from an element shared by the nuances surrounding "humiliation" in the first sentence and the rhetorical function of the negative declaration, a sort of putdown, in the second. In each instance what is expressed is a power relation in which one party is assigned a sense of worthlessness. Yet this relation, precisely because in the first sentence it fails to specify an object (such as poetry), does not reinforce our original reading. The sense which it conveys, instead, is of a unity between sentences at some level not yet articulated. What is thus foregrounded is therefore both a synthetic, contradictory reading and an awareness of the untenable nature of this contradiction. Dramatic tension has been established, not at the level of plot, but between possible readings.

"The ocean/Does not mean to be listened to," finally brings the terms of the first two sentences into an explicit relation. Yet, it also subverts any attempt at straightforward interpretative reading. We have been told that "No one listens to poetry," *not* that poetry means to be listened to. The distinction is significant—by denying that the ocean means to be listened to, the opposition established between ocean and poetry in the two previous sentences (reinforced here by the reiteration of a word from each) requires a reading in which the absent term *poetry* does possess this intentionality. Anthropomorphised without representation, poetry, which "No one listens to," is a figure of impotence, the opposite of "Tougher than anything." The polarity is strengthened by the fact that the ocean occurs as a noun only in the syntactic position of the *subject*, whereas poetry, the noun, is the *object* within a prepositional phrase in the predicate position of a sentence whose subject is "No one."

Spicer's writing here proceeds by negation, by the registration of a difference. At its best, his work can be dizzying: the reader has a difficult time keeping in mind which term initiated a sequence of such negations. This not only serves Spicer's critique of presence, but also follows from his training in linguistics.

Nor is it unusual for there to be devices which are so minute that their impact is perceptible only in the aggregate. His use of overdetermination and self-contradiction is so complicated as to deny a clear sense to the reader—or at least a reader who is not willing to submit the text to microscopic analysis—as to why the poem *feels* so intense, so upsetting, so intuitive, so irrational. This minuteness of device is essential to the opacity, or mystery of Spicer's poetry. The reader feels the small semantic shifts between the non-human subject "This ocean" and the anthropomorphised connotations of "humiliating," just as she feels the great gap between the first two sentences. But those subtler movements are far less likely to be perceived, especially under the conditions by which most poetry is consumed, once over rapidly.

A differentiation needs to be made here between device and effect. A device, insofar as it can be said to be "a thing," is capable of being described. It is as material as any set of vocal or graphic signifiers. An effect (a term analogous to "signified" in linguistics) can be an aggregate of numerous devices, operating at very different levels of perceptibility. An effect can therefore be overdetermined (i.e., self-contradictory, ambiguous, opaque or "natural"). A device, not being an aggregate, cannot. This would explain how specific devices can yield very different effects. For example, variable capitalization and enjambment are used by Judy Grahn to make her poetry appear as "artless plainspeaking," but in the work of Charles Bernstein they are the self-conscious and ironic scars of a bourgeois "high art" commitment to difficulty.

The play between minute device and overdetermined effect continues through Spicer's poem. "A drop/Or crash of water" goes beyond the exemplification of "oceanness." Foregrounded as the first word of a line, "Or" is a *con*junction expressing *dis*junction, the syntactic and semantic functions standing in absolute opposition. By itself, the distinction would be trivial. Here, however, it acquires the status of a device. It is not just that this contradiction of function parallels the opposition between ocean and poetry, between meaning and intention. The internal oppositionality of the word "Or" itself reduplicates the very anti-logic which underlies virtually every other device of the poem. Meaning in this work is negative not simply in the sense of being differential: meaning *is* negation. There shall be no diction without *contra*diction.

Nor are the terms "drop" and "crash" equivalent. The most obvious contrast is in scale, but more crucial is the fact that "drop" is as apt to be an index of quantity as it is of sound. (Consider the alternate "drip.") The reverse is not even remotely possible for "crash." The two terms are incommensurate. Spicer reinforces this contrast not merely through an opposition of consonants (the closed *p* of "drop" against the *sh* of "crash"), nor even through placing one on either side of the line break, but most dramatically through their relation to the prepositional phrase "of water." Perhaps it could be argued that the phrase is made necessary by the grammatical incompleteness of the sentence combined with the broad referential possibilities (vagueness) of "crash." But "drop" and "crash" combine syntactically with "of water" at very different distances, a spatial distinction which is heightened by the use of the line break.

None of these devices is unusual. What is rare is the degree to which they come into play simultaneously, and are organized around a fundamentally linguistic perception: that a statement of such surface symmetry as "A drop/Or crash of water" can in fact be built upon, *and convey*, imbalance and opposition. Consider how differently these same words would read if "Or" appeared prior to the line break. That simple revision would cancel many, if not most, of the functions of this sequence.

Spicer's use of the line break is semantic, as distinct from prosodic or projective. Spicer, unlike many of his generation, demonstrates little concern with the use of the text to construct a credible facsimile of speech. In fact, one has to go back to William Carlos Williams' *Spring & All* to find a use of the line break as devoted to nuances of meaning.

Spicer's focus on the semantic function of the line break along with his creation of meaning through negation, amounts to a sort of structural super-irony, a nihilist's assault on the conventions of line and meaning. This stance is evident in the next sentence, "It means/Nothing." Position within a free verse line weights individual words differently (not unlike the different quanta of power one finds in the seemingly identical squares of a chessboard). With "It means/Nothing," Spicer appears to be rubbing the reader's nose in his negative vision: "means" and "Nothing" could hardly be positioned for greater stress. "It" is also placed for maximum emphasis, occurring after an off-centered caesura. This position combines with the hard "t" (reiterated from "water") to give "It" an unexpected stress. If most sentences in English can be represented as ensembles of words ranked hierarchically through syntax, this one counters that process, according each term great weight. The declarative structure presents syntax, if not language itself, at its most oppressive, admitting no possibility of difference or doubt. All the control and power of meaning reside with the speaker. Naked in their manipulations, declarative sentences reveal the degree to which all language use represents a struggle. Like sex, language is about power. Power over production and consumption of meaning. Spicer uses this supposed act of "direct communication" as the dimension through which to deny meaning itself.

The laying on of devices within this sentence does not stop here. The individual words, "It," "means," and "Nothing," are virtually generic ciphers, without external reference. The three words function like concentric rings of thwarted referentiality: if language is conceived of as a medium, a model that Spicer often turns to in the figure of the poet as radio, it is a medium in the sense of a membrane, as capable of blocking the real as it is of letting it in.

Which is why the meaning "It" is so crucial. What does "It" refer to? The pronoun here is an anaphor, the one point in the sentence capable of admitting exterior content, of establishing context. Anaphor is a Greek term, meaning "carrying back," with two distinct applications in literature. One, derived from linguistics, identifies terms which refer the reader or listener to prior antecedents for their context and meaning. The other, derived from rhetoric, identifies the use of repetition which is characteristic of parallel construction. The word "It" here, and in the poem overall, is endowed with both modes of anaphor. No other word is as critical to the construction of the whole than "It."

"It" means nothing. "It" has no referent, is skewed, indeterminate, off-balance, irreducible. And then, in a dramatic reversal: "It/Is bread and butter/Pepper and salt." Exactly at the point where what should be anticipated is meaninglessness, absence, nothingness and denial, anaphor asserts unfettered presence and nourishment.

Still, "It" has become overdetermined, by virtue of anaphor, contradiction, and its isolation on the seventh line. The four items which follow "is," while grammatically acceptable, accent the false equivalences of parallel syntax, comparing the relationships of bread to butter and salt to pepper, relations which are *not* identical.

In "The death/That young men hope for," as with "A drop/Or crash of water," the lack of a main verb or predicate forces an anaphoric reference to the previous sentence. However its contradiction in that context is obvious. To say that "It" here signifies the ocean, or whatever in turn the ocean might serve as a metaphor or cipher for, would trivialize the reading process. What stands revealed is the degree to which the process of the production and consumption of language is built upon sleight-of-hand, the card tricks of syntax. It is not simply a matter of culture versus nature, of reasoned intelligence overwhelmed by a nonrational material universe, an Other. Here the rational itself is seen as *ir*rational, while still attempting to comprehend the *a*rational rationally. The rational *is* irrational.

"Aimlessly/It pounds the shore." The next sentence returns the reader finally to the figure of the ocean, but uses position to lend the word "It," again capitalized, much greater stress than is given to "shore." What "pounds the shore" is as much It-ness, that which "means nothing," as it is any body of water. The nihilistic component here is provided even greater emphasis in the word "Aimlessly." Named and yet anonymous, "It," this no-thing, a figure of nourishment and object of desire, equitable with death, composed solely of contradiction, present only in absence, is outside any possible spectrum of intentionality.

"White and aimless signals," is only the second sentence to occur entirely on one line. Unlike the first, "No one listens to poetry," it neither begins nor ends the line, making it the only one without internal stress. Once again we find terms of very different nature on either side of a conjunction, and the whole is the third instance of a displaced predicate, a reiteration of device that helps the poem to "hang together." If "aimless" asserts a connection to the previous sentence, "signals" refers instead back to the schema of messages "to be listened to," of intentionality.[4]

The word "White," however, is the only index of color or sight in this text. Yet this one adjective of the senses is thematically "unnecessary." Instead, it enters as from another discourse, which is precisely its function: to remind the reader that the poem is an enclosure. One cannot speak of that which lies outside until it comes in.

The final sentence, repeating the second ("No one listens to poetry"), ties the package of the poem up with a rhetorical bow. The reader is returned to the initial question: what is the subject of this poem? An expository logic would suggest the ocean, the schema raised as the subject of the first sentence, and reiterated throughout. In contrast, the term "poetry" never falls into the grammatical position of a subject; both of its appearances are syntactically identical, the apparent opposite of a theme being "developed." There is, however, a more readerly logic, in which "poetry" would be the subject and "This ocean" a metaphor. Yet the metaphor, if it is one, is constituted not by equation, but by negation and contradiction. Does this then mean that everything which is predicated on that curious term "It" is *not* the case with poetry? That poetry means something? But that it is *not* "bread and butter/Pepper and salt"? That it is *not* "The death/That young men hope for"? That, somehow, poetry "pounds the shore" with intentionality, or else doesn't pound it at all? That its "signals" aren't white, or else aren't signals? If, through some convoluted process of metaphor negated, this text is to be taken as an indirect affirmation of poetry, two sentences remain, utterly declarative, to insist on the falsity of this reading: "No/One listens to poetry." It is even possible to see in that last line break the echo of a comma ("No, one listens to . . ."): simultaneous negation and affirmation. Any attempt to rescue reason through a finding of metaphor is ultimately thwarted by this equation's systematic subversion of logic.

No hint of ocean is allowed in this sentence, just as the topic of peotry is absent from the first. Each time "poetry" enters, it does so as from another discourse, an eruption, an interruption. The final sentence, a bald assertion of closure, is cast in different line form from its previous occurrance, emphasizing the negative and making the word "One" as anonymous and inhuman as "It."

"It/Means nothing." This is not only literal, but self-referential. The poem will not reduce itself to an essay in verse, nor to a metaphoric affirmation of poetry, nor even its opposite. "Aimlessly/It pounds the shore," an example only of itself. Virtually every declarative sentence must be taken in two contradictory and never-resolving ways. The four other sentences are each grammatically incomplete, ambivalent in function, never fully subject or predicate.

This internal density, this intensity, is sustained throughout

Language to a degree not matched by any of Spicer's other books. The structural premise of *Magazine Verse*, which ostensibly organizes works into the modes of seven different publications, disperses any such claustrophobic sense of compression. Yet, if Spicer's writing is such an articulate recognition of the discontinuities and lacunae in "rational" discourse, of the gap which exists between language and the (nonlinguistic) universe, why would the most powerful exemplification of this come in a text which *maximizes* internal connections? Why not, for example, go in exactly the opposite direction and write fragments whose *dis*hension would be their essential commitment to form?[5]

Precisely because the point at which this vision becomes perceptible is in the moment of, in the most literal sense, *contra*diction. The unity of *Language* is not one of agreement. Because it proceeds through negation, reversal and overdetermination, its points are made *between* sentences as often as within them. Increasing the density of contradiction, flooding the text with a surfeit of incommensurable meanings, Spicer is able to bring forward a content which might otherwise lie outside of the possibilities of discourse.

"The rational is irrational" is only a small part of this content, which cannot be named without reducing it to that same dominating system of ostensible reason, continuous presence and predictable cause and effect which Spicer subverts.

The terms which he substitutes for this content's name are the "outside" (in the parapsychological sense of a medium "invading" and dictating the poem) and, even more whimsically, "Martians." His own comment on this is:

> Please don't get me wrong. Martian is just a word for X. I am not saying that the little green men are coming in saucers . . . going into my bedroom and helping me to write poetry, and they ain't.[6]

The outside is not simply that which is received by the poem, like a parasite or virus, but that which can never be named ("just a word for X"), because, as Noam Chomsky once observed, that which lies beyond cognitive capacity cannot be spoken of *through* cognitive capacity.[7] To recall the final admonition of Wittgenstein's *Tractatus*, "What we cannot speak about we must pass over in silence." It was Spicer's task and accomplishment as a poet to cause this dimension to become perceptible, however fleetingly, to the reader. One does not find it stated in the poems, so much as *between* the statements in them, via their displacements, negations and reversals.

The serial poem is the basic unit of Spicer's mature writing. Although booklength, this unit is considerably different from the openended modernist epic which extends from the model of Pound's *Cantos*. It is not merely a question of the serial poem's shorter size, but of closure and discreteness. The serial poem develops the internal unities of the book, while in the same moment emphasizing the distinctness of its individual parts. Each work within a serial poem bears its own scar of closure, but also displaces at least a part of its range of reference outside of the individual text. Spicer builds the superstructure in such a fashion as to avoid any instant in which (as often happens both in naive narrative and expository forms), the subject "snaps" into clarity. Even a poem which concludes with the announcement "This is a poem about the death of John F. Kennedy," as the eighth piece in "Thing Language" does, only reverses the reader's expectations, and directs—or jars— her away from the single poem, to the series. From *After Lorca* onward, Spicer found the serial poem particularly suited for the expression of an absent content.

Another level of focus essential to the articulation of his position is the sentence. Spicer's emphasis on the sentence as a compositional unit also becomes visible first in *After Lorca*, but does not become dominant until the third section of *The Heads of the Town*, "A Textbook of Poetry."

In the second section of the book, "A Fake Novel about the Life of Arthur Rimbaud," Spicer is writing primarily in prose for the first time, in a style heavily conditioned by the history of the French prose poem, and cast (with a playfulness that recalls the experimental fiction of Williams Carlos Williams) into a mock narrative format.

The dead are not alive. That is what this unattractive prose wants to stamp out. Once you see an end to it, you believe that the dead are alive.[8]

A paragraph such as this stops just short of creating the kind of contradicting, overdetermined, self-cancelling meanings found in *Language* and *Magazine Verse*. But already Spicer seems to have found that such surfeits of overmeaning are displayed most clearly in prose, which traditionally foregrounds the semantic and logical functions. Notice, for example, the degree to which the concerns that will dominate *Language* are articulated in Chapter VI of Book III, "The Dead Letter Officer," a work which in every other feature could have been composed by Max Jacob:

> Inside every Rimbaud was a ready-made dead-letter officer. Who really mailed the letter? Who stole the signs?
>
> The signs of his youth and his poetry. The way he looked at things as if they were the last things to be alive.
>
> The robes of his office are vague and noble. He has a hat that he wears on his head. His arms are attached to his shoulders.
>
> Our contempt for his is general and is echoed even in the house of the dead. Blood would not appease his ghost which stays in us after we are in the house of the dead. He is in every corpse, in every human life.
>
> He writes poems, pitches baseballs, fails us whenever we have a nerve to need him. Button-molder too, he grows in us like the river of years.[9]

The dead-letter officer serves the same function elsewhere ascribed to Martians or the outside, an absent present, an inherent contradiction. Yet the existence of this phenomenon is confined here within a narrative figure. His contradictions are narrative. When, in the final sentence, Spicer brings in what appears to be material from another discourse, that device he uses to such great effect later, it is grounded by the word "he" and fails to catalyze the reversal of perception, which *is*, in *Language* and *Magazine Verse*, the mark of the outside, the experience of the poem.

In "A Textbook of Poetry," however, Spicer frees himself of the weight of narrative by utilizing the same strategy employed by Williams in *Spring & All*, the pseudo-essay. While "A Textbook" has more of the structure of argumentation than does *Language*—

breaking the logic of exposition is one of the major advantages of dividing that text into seven shorter sections—,it moves much closer to the possibilities of the later work, achieving a writing that Rimbaud might have dreamed of, but certainly never Jacob:

> Built of solid glass. The temple out there in the weeds and California wildflowers. Out of position. A place where we worship words.
>
> See through into like it is not possible with flesh only by beginning not to be a human being. Only by beginning not to be a soul.
>
> A sole worshipper. And the flesh is important as it rubs into itself your soleness. Or California. A division of where one is.
>
> Where one is is in a temple that sometimes makes us forget that we are in it. Where we are is in a sentence.
>
> Where we are this is idiocy. Where we are a block of solid glass blocks us from all we have dreamed of. But this is not where we are we are to meet them.[10]

Spicer's position here and in his final books seems virtually identical, even to the figure of the poet as medium, to that taken by Rimbaud in the letter to Georges Izambard of May 13th, 1871:

> I have realized that I am a poet. It's not my doing at all. It's wrong to say: I think. Better to say: I am thought. Pardon the pun.
> I is somebody else. So what if a piece of wood discovers it's a violin . . .[11]

Only in turning fully to prose was Spicer finally capable of confronting the co-existence of absence within presence in his work, an absence often covered over or hidden in his verse through mimciry of voice or song. From "A Textbook of Poetry" through the end of *Magazine Verse*, Spicer became the first truly sentence-centered poet in the American language.

This does not mean, however, that he worked only in paragraph form. In fact, with the exception of the few doggerel and/or ballad style pieces in his later work, Spicer primarily explored and transformed the relationship between line and sentence. The sentence became the unit of composition, and the line (which is, after all, nothing more than a line-break and the possibility of caesura) a means for locating stress within the sentence. This approach posits stress at places that twist, or even contradict, the apparent denotative meaning. Thus, in "This ocean . . . ," the break in the last sentence, "No/One listens to poetry," foregrounds the anonymity in the word "One." The ghostly dead-letter officer is palpably at home here, more truly absent in his presence than when cast as a narrative figure. From the perspective of the reader the absence is experiential, not merely depicted. Through his line breaks, suppressed verbs and numerous insertions of sentences apparently taken from other discourses, Spicer destabilizes prose even as he takes it as his form. It is precisely in these nooks and crannies, gaps and lacunae that the "outside" is permitted finally to speak.

Spicer's work anticipates many of the developments in poetry over the past twenty years. In this context it is worth noting that Spicer, both as poet and linguist, rather aggressively disputed the valorization of language within the process of the poem. "Words are," he said in Vancouver,

> things which just happen to be in your head instead of someone else's head. . . . The words are counters and the whole structure of language is essentially a counter. It's an obstruction to what the poem wants to do.[12]

Or, earlier in the same talk:

> Creeley talks about poems following the dictation of language. It seems to me that's nonsense—language is part of the furniture of the room. Language isn't anything of itself—it's something which is in the mind of the host, the parasite that the poem is invading—five languages just makes the room structure more difficult and also possibly, more usable. It certainly doesn't have anything to do with any mystique of English or anything else. . . . I prefer more the unknown.[13]

The unknown. That which lies beyond cognitive capacity. That which to attempt to speak of (and here Spicer's occasional forays into the vocabulary of esoteric traditions seems not to work to his advantage) is apt to sound mystical, but is, or should be, exactly not. For it is perceptible between sentences, in the surfeit of incommensurable meanings, in the twists and gaps of sytax and logic. The last sentence of Wittgenstein's *Tractatus*, as Spicer could have told us, is wrong. What we cannot speak about should not be passed over in silence. It remains to be shown.

SENTENCES

Robert Grenier may be better known for his translations (Trakl), his editing (with Barrett Watten, the first three issues of *This* and most recently Creeley's *Selected Poems*), and his impact as a teacher (at Iowa, Berkeley, Tufts, and New College), than he is as a poet. This expensive edition,* limited to 200 copies, is one attempt to alter this circumstance. *Sentences* consists of 500 five-by-eight cards in no particular order (no two boxes are identical), very few of which have more than a dozen words imprinted on them. It can be read as easily as one work as five hundred, and Grenier himself has been careful to give no clues in this regard. These cards present a vision of language which is at once rich, direct, witty, precise and subtle. Some readers, however, might wonder what motivates a one-time student of Robert Lowell into giving the name and prestige of literature to such writings as

later

or

good good

or

s o m e o l d g u y s w i t h s c y t h e s

The answer is that Grenier, much like the Russian formalist critics of the revolutionary period, takes language to be the *issue*

---

*SENTENCES (Whale Cloth Press, 1978), boxed (unbound).

(topic, substance, subject) of poetry: *Sentences* is first of all a display of words as he found them, alive in America in the seventies. Again like the formalists, Grenier takes context (or framing) as the primary factor in the setting up of perception in relation to this topic: the method of *Sentences* (which it shares with much of the visual and performance art of recent years) is persistently the *removal* of context, which accounts for both the minimalism of these pieces and the refusal to order, let alone bind them as "pages."

Inevitably, any project which proceeds in this fashion is going to submerge a lot of its own structuring impulses: some method is necessary for the selection of which language to display; there is also the problem of *microwriting*, the internal dynamics of such miniature units. I want to get at the first issue by initially suggesting a response to the second.

Grenier's obsessive formal concern is with balance. The piece

obtain from the brook

is one example. Its theme is the alphabet, specifically the letters *o, b* and *t*. The work is divided into equal halves, one containing a verb and preposition, the other a noun phrase; in both parts, the vowel occurs twice and the consonants once each—but the phonemes implicated in each instance are radically different, the mute uniformity of the graphemic hiding a scandal of sound. And all contained within a slice of "ordinary" language, the framing itself calling attention to balance, since these words have been taken *off-center* (normally the preposition would link itself "naturally" to the noun phrase, but this is countered by the minimalism, the prosody and the thematic distribution of letters) from what presumably was a larger, grammatically typical utterance some-where in the world.

Balance, which marks Grenier's debt to Zukofsky's Shakes-pearean aspect, is a complex, inclusive focus, bringing in a wide range of metaphysical concerns which are explored through the practical activity of writing. Often, as above, the play is between identity and difference, presence and absence, speech and writing, continuity and discreteness, the potential for reiteration (repetition being a favorite device of Grenier's), and the uniqueness of the particular. Within the zone of free play constituted by these writings, balance is that resolution which accounts for, and even demands, the existence of these seeming contradictions.

Seen from this perspective, the 500 cards might then be grouped or typed. I want to suggest, tentatively and very roughly, one possible breakdown, but before doing so I need to warn that Grenier himself does not proceed analytically, so that what is proposed below should not be taken as a description of intent, but of an emergent structure which reveals itself only accumulatively, in the wake of numerous concrete acts of jotting-it-all-down. Inevitably, a conceptual herding together of materials on this order is going to be impressionistic and arbitrary (many pieces could fit into several categories and, often, *that* is the point), yet even a crude listing of approximate likenesses should identify areas which a serious reader will want to explore for herself.

Simply piling cards into what seems to be the fewest intelligible groupings, I arrive at 16 types, which in turn cluster around two general concerns that parallel the distinction filmmaker Malcom LeGrice makes between compositional and investigatory modes of art. In Grenier's version of the compositional, the issue of balance (and/or presence) dominates the writing; in the investigatory, the emphasis is turned toward the origin of the language chosen, although here also individual works are often constructed around questions of balance. Each type contains five piles of cards. Six other piles seem to share both tendencies to the extent where this mixture (ambivalence, in the strict sense of the word) is the dominant factor.

Composition modes: (1) one-word pieces: a term's presence is set in opposition to the absence of any context whatsoever; (2) pieces where the words run together in a *s p a c e d* typography: the borders of terms dissolve and the presence(s) of letters are foregrounded; (3) two-word pieces (*why fragment, it's you*); (4) three-word pieces (*foot two three*); (5) studies of balance (*twelve to twelve to one*, or *ocean is/ /groceries*).

Investigation modes: (1) individual quotations (all but two from Grenier's daughter and ex-wife); (2) discussions, usually with the voices marked, as in a theater piece, by letters; (3) pieces setting off the discursive function (*these tubes/have been/on the floor*, where the first word being a shifter aims attention toward a deliberately absent discourse); (4) I-pieces (*I drink rice*), all of which are statements skewed by that primary shifter; (5) multiple statements (*by then your clothes are very wrinkled//worse than that I'm hard at work*), several of which, by their size, turn into little poems and/or songs.

Mixed modes: (1) pieces where titles, in caps, oppose texts (the problematics here typify the mixed mode: opposition is one type of balance, yet the function of title most often sets these pieces off as of-the-poetic); (2) studies of *im*balance, slices of linguistic life made by nonorthodox cuts (*yawns at solid*); (3) totalities, completed statements and/or images (*the sidewalk is for pedestrians*): origin and balance achieve symbiosis here; (4) errata, such as spoonerisms (*Friday home you stayed night and sewed*): here imbalance is *at* the origin; (5) the graphemic (*39/ground /ɇ/huck*): the presence of the reading mind's voice here is a supplement, a reminder of its own distance from the ink of print; (6) pieces in which the alienism in words floods over (*SMILES///see me i ill aisles miles smile smiles//less*).

Within each type, even each piece, there's a great deal of play (putting *I drink rice* in a slot doesn't begin to explore what's at work there), plus Grenier's remarkably developed sense for what is *actually said*, rather than what is heard, in any conversation. The total impact—one can read the entire box in an hour—is massive. *Sentences* drenches us in the present fact of our own language. As such, its scope is panoramic on a scale not dreamed of since Whitman.

CONTROLLING INTERESTS

> The category of the subject is constitutive
> of all ideology.
>
> — Louis Althusser

I

> Poetry has for the moment assumed the position formerly occupied by
> philosophy.
>
> — Laura Riding

The problem of poetry at the end of the 20th century is who shall write it, not in the sense of which persons, but rather persons *of what order?* How will they be constituted, understand their own "individuality," and relate this to such audiences as each attempts to construct? Such questions are both literary and social.

Since the 1760s of Jupiter Hammon and Phyllis Wheatley, there have been two literatures in the United States, one of them conscious of, and directed toward (most often from within), the social movements of dominated groups. The marginality of this oppositional tradition has been both attested to, and reinforced, by the studied silence accorded it by the apparatuses of a seemingly larger literary "center": the universities, journals, publishers, libraries, writers and readers of the hegemonic culture. For good reason, those who participate in the legitimating mechanisms of the dominant literature have seldom perceived themselves as bearing an explicit relationship to any social or historical movement. On those occasions when this connection has been made, the term by which these agents identify their own cause has been (and is) invariably universalist, such as freedom, rather than descriptive and specific, such as capitalism. This claim to universalism in turn serves to justify a process by which the writing of the dominated is discounted. Because the relation of art to society within these two realms is different, and thus because the aesthetic needs which oppositional poetry attempts to meet are not shared by those who govern the major institutions of literary legitimation (precisely while those values which they do hold may be absent, if not directly challenged), it appears obvious and natural, at least to some, that the poetry of subaltern constituencies (women, sexual, ethnic or linguistic minorities, the working class and its historic descendants, etc.) should be inherently peripheral. This perspective is further buttressed by the dominant literary community's sense of its own completeness. Through systematic token representation, it can include and contain all types of difference. Universalism not only marginalizes, but also accounts for the status of those to whom it has done this in terms which would appear to be neutral and value-free.

Of course, neither the poetry of the center nor those of the peripheries are in any real sense homogenous. Rather than a struggle between clearly defined alternatives, we find instead ensembles of values which may overlap as much as they conflict with one another. In a case such as Hart Crane, for example, it is not difficult to demonstrate a direct clash within the work of a single poet or even a single poem. These are complexities which have only been heightened in our time by a shift that is still taking place between these various traditions, one caused primarily by the coming into consciousness *as dominated groups* of significant numbers of people due to the sexual and labor reconfigurations of society since the Second World War. This is most visible perhaps with regard to the women's movement, but the phenomenon has been much more far reaching. The result has been a decentralization in which any pretense, whether from the "center" or elsewhere, of a coherent sense as to the nature of the whole of American poetry is now patently obvious as just so much aggressive fakery. The entire spatial metaphor of center and periphery is thus a model whose major function is to mask hierarchy.

This is not to suggest that literary hierarchies do not exist, only that their origins are social. In fact, in coming to recognize the existence of such hierarchies as essential to any understanding of the social organization of literature itself, what has emerged as inherent within any writing is its connection to a determinate audience, a collectivity which is never universal—and which may be subject to identification, description and analysis. Acts which, in the poet's hand no less than in the political operative's, are mechanisms for use in a struggle over social (or self) determination and control. Poetry, like war, is the pursuit of politics by other means. For the writing of the dominated, particularly in the present moment, this relationship between text and context may be expressed more or less directly. To identify oneself, and especially one's reader, as anything other than a white male heterosexual of a certain education and class background is, after all, to directly counter the most pervasive of universalist presumptions. But what about the other tradition, one which has by no means been produced entirely by whites, males or heterosexuals? To argue that to engage "bourgeois" writing is to necessarily align oneself on the side of its cause or social movement, capitalism, not only is to reduce individuals to the category of oppressor by virtue of their race, gender, sexuality or class background, but fails to account for the multitude of ways in which these persons also experience powerlessness in a hierarchical society. To the contrary, the processes by which the counter-traditions have decentralized American poetry have revealed the dominant literature to be a variegated terrain. And while it may very well tend toward the same vertical organization through which it reflects and reproduces the dynamics of the larger society, the positions on this particular map are not fixed. In this respect also, bourgeois poetry mimics the instability of a market-driven economy.

These are the circumstances which confront any poet today who either falls, or chooses to work, within the tradition of the dominant literature. It should not be surprising, therefore, that precisely the issue which so thoroughly and directly defines difference, and thus identity, has become a major point of contention between bourgeois poets: who is the subject, that "I" which both speaks and reads the text? If it is not Universal Man, as surely it is not, what then is the nature of this beast? Until this is answered, all further considerations of the relationship within this terrain between poem and audience must be deferred for lack of sufficient information. Yet it equally follows that there can be no such thing as a formal problem in poetry which is not a social one as well. It is no longer a matter, say, of what makes for a good linebreak, but rather how a specific device conditions a reader to respond, to identify as a subject of a particular type—and of the position and fate of this type within history. Thus the off-balance, breath-imitating line of the Black Mountain poets, especially Robert Creeley and the early Charles Olson, foregrounds the presence of a speaker by setting up a physiological distinction between that persona and the internal rhythms of the reader. Such prosodic stylization restricts the audience's ability to identify with the expository voice of the text, freeing them to observe (or even judge) the experience from the position of their own extra-literary lives. This respect for the separateness and integrity of the consumer is lost when a dramatic monologue is constructed by means of normative syntax, classical metrics and a deliberately recessive linebreak—devices that render the reading subject passive and unaware of their own presence. Regardless of the announced politics of such a poem, which might be anything, its fundamental commitment at the level of the reader's experience is to passivity, to the subject which can only observe, incapable of action.

For those poets working within the bourgeois tradition who choose to confront the myth of universalism, the capacity of language to constitute a subject (that self which, in the most literal sense, asserts and experiences subjectivity) has become a major field of investigation. Language's ability to constitute, to generate meaning and models, to imply psychological structures, and to represent, and interact with, the universe of non-linguistic experience, however, has historically been the domain of another profession: philosophy. It should not be surprising, therefore, that we should have a book of poems such as *Controlling Interests*, composed by a poet, Charles Bernstein, trained originally as a philosopher.

The positivism which underlies the universalist claim within any given discourse, such as poetry, protects itself by relegating all difference elsewhere, seeking to maintain an absolute division between fields not unlike the jealous guarding of borders between academic departments on a college campus. Bernstein, in an essay entitled "Writing and Method," challenges this, arguing that:

what makes poetry poetry and philosophy philosophy is largely a tradition of thinking and writing, and a social matrix of publications, professional associations, audience; more, indeed, facts of history and social convention than intrinsic necessities of the "medium" or "idea" of either one.[1]

"Writing and Method" makes much of the interchangeability of the value claims implicit in both poetry and philosophy *as practices*. What is at issue is not the idealization or abstraction of either discipline, so much as their common containment within language. If an investigation of the construction of subjects through language is to be the project of writing, an approach which demands an accompanying critique of universalism and positivism, what better strategy might there be than to integrate and consciously bastardize those professions for which language itself has traditionally been conceived of as both medium and outer limit? Nevertheless, Bernstein's hybrid attack is biased on the side of poetry. His stance enables him to "liberate" philosophy from its context of professional pedantry by prefering the decentralized, economic marginality of poetry as the discourse through which to proceed.

If this is not always evident in *Controlling Interests*, it is because Bernstein's books, unlike much contemporary poetry, are organized thematically, rather than chronologically. In earlier volumes, such as *Poetic Justice*, published in 1979, this has meant that individual pieces of considerably different capacity and completeness sit juxtaposed. But even in more recent texts, as in *Interests* or *Islets/Irritations*, an unevenness is both apparent and deliberate.

Disrupting chronology is a defense against the reduction of poetry to "mere" autobiography, particularly when the formation of a subject is taken as the persistent content of the work. Bernstein employs his temporally fragmented authorial subject, in turn, as an instrument to pierce the veil of "pure abstraction" characteristic of modern philosophy. Focusing on the constitutive aspect of language, rather than treating it as a self-forming *object* (as did Wittgenstein), Bernstein grounds the medium in its relation to an external world, a terrain which is neither permanent nor complete. If, like the book, each poem in *Controlling Interests* can be read as a meditation or essay, these arguments proceed by means of discontinuous units, many of which can stand as a critique or challenge to the whole.

II

> For love—I would
> split open your head and put
> a candle in
> behind the eyes.
>
> Love is dead in us
> if we forget
> the virtues of an amulet
> and quick surprise.
> — Robert Creeley
> *The Warning*[2]

"For Love Has Such A Spirit That If It Is Portrayed It Dies" is one of the ten (of 17) poems in *Controlling Interests* to employ the form of a single, long stanza composed of medium length (or larger) lines. Three of the other poems are in prose, three in a modified field technique which seems highly conscious of its ancestry (Berrigan/Waldman in the case of "Off Season" and "The Hand Gets Scald . . . ," Eigner in "Company Life"), with one, "Standing Target," in a mixed mode. Of the stanzaic pieces eight have simple titles: Matters of Policy," "Sentences My Father Used," "Island Life," etc. One has no title other than its first line, and one, "For Love," a title so elaborate as to call attention to itself.

This last title uses the rhetorical mode of an assertion, such as might be taken up by a speaker as a topic for debate. The discourse genre, or frame, of "For Love" is literally that of exposition.

> Mass of van contemplation to intercede crush of
> plaster. Lots of loom: "smoke out", merely
> complicated by the first time something and don't.
> Long last, occurrence of bell, altitude, attitude of.[3]

In a formal argument, these opening lines would identify the thesis, or a recitation of the problem; in a natural narrative, this would be moment of orientation.[4] In one sense, a minor one, these lines do present, or at least exemplify, "the problem," the dangers of material reality ("crush of/plaster") in an air of anxiety, confusion, hesitation. This is a *dis*orientation, achieved by extreme condensation and fragmentation of language: there is an irony which comes across as doubting in the use of a word such as "van"

176

(whose first meaning in the Random House Collegiate is essentially "short for *vanguard*") to characterize a contemplation capable of keeping the sheetrock from one's brow. More sinister, "loom" in the second line can carry two very different meanings, neither of which is reducible to an aspect of the other. The use of quotation marks furthers this, setting words off as from "another voice," failing to *resolve* with the comma into an integrated, conventional punctuation. "Smoke" carries the connotation of a dust projected (not written) from the falling plaster—but this meaning, tangible as it is, is not possible in "smoke out." A parallel frustration occurs in the next line in the ellipsis hidden by "something," about which we are only told "and don't." Beyond the alliterative echo to "Lots of loom," "Long last" (like "loom") presents different possible readings, in this instance both contractions, from either "Long lasting" or "at long last." Perversely, "occurrence of bell" (not to be confused with its sound) suggests the latter without any further evidence of connection. A relation to the bell is similarly *projected by context* onto "altitude, attitude of" in the same instant that those first two words, by virtue of their acoustics, mark rhyme (an "occurrence of bell"), while suggesting through spelling a typographical error (and yet attitude, in the sense of position, would be determined partly by altitude). Disordered or random as these four lines might appear, they represent an intensely controlled, polysemic and subtle act of writing.

This level of discrimination is characteristic of Bernstein's mature work. While I won't pursue the reading to this degree of detail, the devices, movements and themes which follow warrant comment. In the next passage, tone and surface shift:

> The first, at this moment, aimless, *aims*. To the
> point of inordinate asphalt—lecture, entail.
> These hoops regard me suspiciously. A ring
> for the should (heave, sigh . . .). Broadminded in
> declamation, an arduous task of winking
> (willing). Weary the way the world wearies,
> circa 1962. The more adjoins, sparklet and parquet
> reflection, burned out (up). Regard the willing,
> whose movement be only remonstration, ails
> this blue bound boat. The numberical tears.

Some of the techniques employed to accomplish this shift are already familiar: ellipsis (the first *what*, the more *what?*), and alliteration—especially in the sixth and tenth lines—used to deflect and divert "literal" meaning (it is the *b* in "numberical" that "tears," sounded as it must be, failing to become numb, absent). What distinguishes this passage's ostensible clarity from the initial quatrain is that, with the possible exception of "hoops," no words or phrases are stranded between determinate, irreducible content. Which is not to say that several words do not have multiple meanings, but rather that such meanings are ordered: the layered idiom of "burned out (up)" carries, in context, more of exhaustion and frustration than it does of fire, and hence of any reference back to "smoke;" the same is true for the relation between "Ring" and "bell." Nor do any of the terms portend disaster as did "crush" and "smoke." There are several allusions, treated descriptively as from a third person, to modes and tropes of argumentation itself: "lecture," "declamation," "remonstration." The two sides of any communicative social contract are visible in the sentence "These hoops regard me suspiciously" and the phrase "winking/(willing)," the first suggesting that the contract is only tenuously held ("hoops" is not a metaphor, but a cipher inserted in the place of an ellipsis), the second marking the gap between signifier and signified. Finally, sentences proceed, in contrast with those of the first four lines, as if from one to the next: *"aims.* To the/point of."

The effect of these last lines, syllogistic flow, Bernstein in "Writing and Method," calls *projection:* that act of the reading mind which interprets new words, phrases and sentences as possessing the *least disjunctive* meaning. While the effect of this phenomenon is to minimize the recognition of gaps and changes in context, content or scale, Bernstein takes it in the opposite direction, making tangible to the reader the act of projection itself, an (unwilling) participation to locate meaning(s) which she knows no "literal" interpretation could support. This is the antithesis of modernism's "hidden meanings," in that its content is the *hiding process.*

> Edged out where tunnels reconnect, just below
> the track. Aims departing after one another
> & you just steps away, listening,
> listless. Alright, always—riches
> of that uncomplicated promise. Who— what—

that this reassurance (announcement)
& terribly prompted—almost,
although. Although censorious and even more
careless. Lyrical mysticism—harbor, departing
windows. For love I would—deft equator.
Nonchalant attribution of all the, & filled with
such, meddles with & steals my constancy, sharpening
desire for that, in passing, there, be favorite
in ordinary, but no sooner thought than gone. My
heart seems wax, that like tapers burns at light.
Fabulous ephemera a constant force for giddy flight.

Here the modes of stoppage, prosody's (and punctuation's) markings of hesitation, multiply. Words to which any material visual referent might be applied dwindle. Concrete referents occur in only three sentences: the first (a complex, but not impossible, image), the tenth (a romanticized and ironic simile, undermined by a disagreement in number and inversion of cause and effect) and the seventh, where they are characterized as "Lyrical mysticism." The infamous shifter "You," with a content different for every reader, is objectified by the use of the verb in the third person, a descriptive conjugation. What remains is nearly all (unfinished) mental constructs and the gears of syntax, a reading experience in which language is posed as a *barrier* to actuality. Not only is this passage filled with implied ellipsis, terms bearing negative connotations ("listless," "censorious," "careless," "mysticism," "meddles with," "steals") further depress the whole. Into this are set a smaller number of words and phrases with a directly opposite emotional coding: "riches/of that uncomplicated promise," "reassurance," "desire," "favorite," and, at least on one level, "For love." The result is a strobe effect of charged connotations ("no sooner thought than gone"), unrelieved by either concrete imagery or the simple pleasure of a completed thought—until the last two sentences, which go to the point of end-rhyme to mark the counterpoint of their harmony. While the first of these two sentences is pointedly comic, the second is not, stating what the poem heretofore has exemplified: the problem of projection, actuality and action.

The demand for spontaneous intersubjectivity, which is at the heart of Creeley's "The Warning," presents a possible reading of Bernstein's project. Like the Creeley poem, which is itself "about" frustration, Bernstein here recognizes the impotency of this demand: the allusion is abruptly broken in the most radical instance of stoppage in this section, followed by a long, lax sentence composed of disconnected strands. The reference to Creeley (and by this to a whole tradition of writing and proposed solutions) also serves to rewrite, midway through the text, the title of Bernstein's piece, so that love itself is no longer *portrayed*, save through the mediation of another text.[5]

> But boxes both in, boated just the same. Mass of fix,
> the further theorizing a final surrender, until the next, thins
> or becomes transported, nights asleep, days wondering.
> Appearance that not so much won't shake but returns, as
> the pilot turns his starship into wool. To knit
> these phantasmagorias out of white, sheer monument to culture's
> merry meal of itself. In eyes that look with mirror's blankness,
> remoteness complete—I want but all recedes. Motor
> fixation, streetcar trace, the last days of this
> water, these fields. To sustain such blows and
> undermine the lash is memory's cure. At long
> last, image reconciled to friend, chatting
> under oaks, rays of a sky no longer our
> but all the more possessed. For much that has
> no cure. Duplication equal to charm of happier times, those that
> disappeared, faster and more fantastic, the loud
> despair the softer homily. A shoe entails
> its path till, foot on foot, no diversion's
> seen. The sky parts, the blinds repair.
> A hush that skirts the subtler moment,
> the cumbersome charade of weekend and reply.

Continuing the strategy begun in the last sentence of the previous passage, the language here largely presents an argument rather than exemplifying a condition or state. The shift is dramatic, with consequences on multiple levels. With the exception of "I want but all recedes," ellipses virtually disappear, replaced by a variety of other devices, notably synecdoche, used to torque, condense and intensify the discourse. A more fluent prosody is constructed by greatly decreasing the frequency of full stops. Because of the structure of argument itself, syllogistic flow is increased, displacing the reader's sense of projection onto the tropes with the sentences. In contrast with the discontinuous-but-eternal presentness that characterizes much "new sentence" writing, several of the terms are pointedly anaphoric, referring back to previous occurrences.

What is at issue here is the constant *re*formation of the subject, isolated and idealized behind a wall of language that presents a *false* picture. This invalidness is as much the content of all the subversions of expectation (blinds don't repair any more than the sky parts) as it is the lost possession of the sky, an instance of memory curing "much that has/ no cure." At its most material, this reformed (falsified) subject perceives the "weekend" as a base and the workweek its "reply."

Bernstein is rejecting analysis ("further theorizing a final surrender"), intersubjectivity ("eyes that look with mirror's blankness," exactly the problem posed by Creeley's "The Warning," "remoteness complete"), and memory as roads out of the vicious circle of language's ideological solipsism. None offers a means for relocating the unfalsified subject, our "true selves." At best they intensify our consciousness of the difficulty. This is explicit in the lines which follow:

This darkness, how richer than a moat it lies. And
my love, who takes my hand, now, to watch all this
pass by, has only care, she and I. We deceive
ourselves in this matter because we are in
the habit of thinking the leaves will fall or
that there are few ways of breaking the circuit.

In spite of the directness of statement, the tone here is fully ironic, comically at first, then more ominously in that last, long sentence. In it alienation is complete: that the leaves will fall is *not* a "habit of thinking." The irony is reinforced by the fact that the sentence is the first in the poem to be grammatically complete and conventional, and seemingly as normative at the level of content. Seemingly, because the last line presents a variety of possible readings which neither the sentence nor the remainder of the poem resolve (yet is not "breaking the circuit" what this is all about?):

How much the stronger we would have been had
not—but it is something when one is lonely
and miserable to imagine history on your side. On

the stoop, by the door ledge, we stand here, coffee
in hand. Roll top desk, undisguised goodbyes. I
wait but I don't want it. Austerely premature,
scrutinized to the point of a gazeless graph, no past
there, how could it hope to mean to us. These
are the saccharine days, the noiseless
chirps of the sublimated depths. By the train
tracks, halfway down, sitting there, looking at—
a goat knows no better sound. What of colors, what
of characters—anoint with all precision
projection brings, so much sturdier and
valorous than ourselves. Depressed eyes
clutter the morning and we drown in a sea of
helping hands. Better the hermit than the sociopath.
Destruction? —the wind blows anyway, any where,
and the window frame adorns the spectacle. That
person fixes in your head, and all the world
consumed through it.

By now the close reader should be able to pursue the poem very
nearly as straightforward argument, in spite of increases in ellipses
and stoppage, and the disruptions of syllogistic flow through the
insertion of a number of imagized sentences. The proximity here of
not wanting to "a gazeless graph" is in direct contrast to the earlier:

In eyes that look with mirror's blankness,
remoteness complete—I want but all recedes

indicating a movement in position that might be interpreted as a
zen-like "letting go" of the dilemma, but is followed by yet another
reformation of the problem framed finally in the most negative
terms: "how could it hope to mean to us," "saccharine days,"
"noiseless chirps," "Depressed eyes clutter," "drown," "hermit,"
"sociopath," and even "Destruction?," posed as a question whose
lack of an answer is deafening. False though it might be, and
imposed from the outside ("That/person"), the subject is
nonetheless the vehicle or lens through which "all the world" is not
so much experienced as "consumed." By its placement, this last
sentence offers neither alternative, nor escape, nor solace.
    Beyond the initial gestures of argumentation per se, and the
discrete instances of standing, sitting, looking at, watching and,
significantly, "takes my hand," the most concrete act before "we
drown" is that "the pilot turns his starship into wool." The final

designation of eyes as "Depressed," the figure of the window, and the nearly catatonic passivity of anything resembling the instance of a character show Bernstein unwilling to prescribe a strategy of response. At no moment in this poem (or elsewhere in *Controlling Interests, Senses of Responsibility, Poetic Justice* or *Shade*) is action proposed, let alone valorized, as an antidote to that subjective transformation of material reality through language which converts the social relations of everyday life into a paralyzing pseudonature. In "Writing and Method," however, Bernstein does suggest a relation between the poem and "the hierarchical power relations within the socious," when he calls for:

> Writing as a map for the reader to read into, to interpolate from the space of the page out onto a projected field of "thinking". . . . So that the meaning of the text is constituted only in collaboration with the reader's active construction of this hypertext. This construction by the reader transforms the text in a way analogous to a stereopticon's transformation of two photoslides, except that the final construction is not uniform with each reader/viewer. . . .
> (. . . what I am discussing brings to consciousness the fact of projection as part of the content. . . .)
> . . . it is the formal autonomy of the text as model that elicits a response, an interpolation.[6]

Conceived as such, poetry is part of a larger, oppositional strategy and cannot be viewed as an end in itself (even as the poet insists on the necessary "autonomy of the text"). The function of a writing so proposed would be to make the reader aware of the role of projection *as a response to form* in the constitution of the reader as a subject—and always as a subject of a specific type, as one who reads poetry in a nation where it is not much read, and who selects a specific poetry to read.

Implied within this formulation (although not named by Bernstein) is the outline of a particular audience. At its most general, it is that group which historically has not been conscious of its own existence *as a group*, that is, the dominant, or "un-marked" class. Without self-awareness (apart from recognized, shared, class interests) or a reflexive nature, this audience is most at risk of perceiving themselves—and the formulation of themselves as subjects—as *inevitable*" (such solipsism is perhaps most grossly evident in American exceptionalism in its many forms, but is also the presumption underwiting all lines of racist, sexist, ageist and classist thought). More narrowly defined, this audience of possible readers is that portion of the larger group which *has* (have) begun to come into awareness of its (their) participation within a group. For this section of bourgeois poetry, the recognition of the construction of the individual through ideology, by means of language and other codes, is not an intellectual game. This new awareness is a matter of survival with deeply personal dimensions.

Critical poetry such as Bernstein's, which wrests these issues from the academic domain of professional philosophy, and which roots the problem of the formation of subjects in the reader's response to form, is not the only poetry which is being written (or needs to be written) in the United States today. And certainly these questions themselves extend well beyond the boundaries of poetry or philosophy. But, to the degree that an oppositional movement within bourgeois poetics reflects a similar fissure within the bourgeoisie itself—an opposition whose goal is not domination of class, but an end to all relations of power predicated upon human difference, those "controlling intersts"—this is a poetry which demands our attention. It exists not to be appreciated, but to be understood.

184

HANNAH WEINER

These works* represent a major departure from *Clairvoyant Journal* the long prose "diary" for which Hannah Weiner is best known. What comment there has been on her writing has focused largely on the claim to clairvoyance, specifically on the capacity to *see words* figured with the qualities of light or of such substances as pencils or dog fur. Such comment tends to obscure the essential fact that these works *are writing*, literary productions rigorously following all the demands posed by the questions of their composition to a unique and rich result. For example, the very multiplicity of voices in the *Journal* explores the problem of the constitution of an authorial subject as fully as the analytical/exemplificative strategy used by Charles Bernstein in *Controlling Interests*, the deconstruction through form of Lyn Hejinian's *My Life* or the intersubjective reversals that Steve Benson builds into the pronouns of *Blindspots*. And by its very status as "diary" the *Journal* insists, even more clearly than does Hejinian, that this issue is not simply a problem of contemporary existential intellectualism, but is compellingly at the center of our lives.

The *Journal* also engages such issues as representation, narrative, continuity versus simultaneity, the directionality of the line, the page (*specifically* the 8½ x 11 inch page) as compositional space or stanza, and the function of prosody within prose. The interruptions imposed on the text by the inclusion of "seen words" work to break the flow of syntax and thought more powerfully than a space will break a line, yielding a "thought fragment" as a measure of quantity, simultaneously enabling the inclusion of multiple

---

Little Books/Indians. (Roof, 1980).
 Nijole's House. (Potes & Poets Press, 1981).

narrative/expository/discursive threads in a manner which becomes utterly readable once the reader gives herself *permission* to make active decisions in the consumption of the text. In no other recent work is the reader's place as collaborator as tangible as it is in the *Journal.*

In *Little Books/Indians* and *Nijole's House,* Weiner returns to the poem as form, i.e., the line, (although still informed by the inclusion of "other" data, a doubling therefore of the interruptive process which linebreaks place at the heart of prosody). And yet, as she states in "Little Book 115: Virgin," these works are considered by her to be "prose," just as she has elsewhere referred to the *Journal* as a "novel." All writing makes present to its readers the intense activities of the mind, although some genres, such as journalism and "realist" fiction, tend to efface the traces which lead back to the author. In fact, it is precisely the existence of genre, purely a social convention, which carries any finished text *away*, however small a distance, from the presentness of activity, as such. We might say, therefore, that genre erases the assertion of an authorial subject. From this perspective, Weiner's ambivalences, displacements and disruptions of genre form (to the extent that, in some places "t"s are not crossed or the top portions of words disappear) reinforce her critique of the voices which operate through her to construct "a self."

Of the poems or prose works in *Little Books/Indians* the only one short enough to quote here by way of example is "Little Book 138 Pedro   April 30 79," which is among the least disruptive typographically. Like most of the little books (so called because the original versions were composed in the 29¢ "pocket memos" from which the volume derives its cover design), this piece begins from an event out of Weiner's experience working with the American Indian Movement, the incarceration of Leonard Crow Dog:

THEY TOOK ME
into a prison cell
& tormented me
for quite a while

LEONARDS STORY

I ams chained
WHO BELIEVES IT
       MARY DOES
she can feel
the pinches
BIG TOE HEALS
Leonard's prison term

stupid dear an old
crime
He was tormented stupid
and I THREW IT UP
because he couldnt
THAS A TRICK
write for Big Deal
now one week
lost
SOS I SPEAK

WHO CHEATS
       amongst the Indians
            SIS IM SCARED
Only a Guru can
CHEAT LIKE LEONARD
he's full of shit too
caress him
HANNAH STOP
WRITING IT IN

This is very nearly a meditation on the old line about poetry being a
"kind of lie," that would permit one to see the truth more clearly.
Although Weiner often seems to describe her composition/
transcription practice otherwise, it appears evident that the
disruption of voices and the disruption of typography are not
identical. In fact, this divergence gives Weiner one set of rhythms
based on the ear, or at least syntax, and another based on the eye.
The multiplicity of voices often gives particularly charged terms,
such as *CHEATS*, an increased sense of instability, since it is not
evident what the relation of intention between the writer and the
term might be. Weiner adds to this volatile affect by undermining
the typographic integrity of individual words, a device which is
associated in this piece with the presence of "s." This sets up the

several meanings of *SOS* (so, help, and, three lines later, *SIS*), an instance of more than one "voice" inhabiting a single term. The "unstable s" also permits Weiner the irony of elegance in the word *amongst* in the same passage.

Just how far the *Little Books* differ from the address of the *Journal* is best registered, I suspect, by the presence of the "I". This is a discourse posed to an Other far more than the "diary" mode of the earlier work (in which the author must also inhabit the role of "a reader"). Perhaps this also explains the use of the poetic line, in which a stop is marked not by the presence of other information but by a graphic silence. Typographically, the first two sections of this volume represent Weiner's most extreme investigation of word and line without ever falling into the stasis of "concrete" poetry.

Nijole's House is an extended writing in verse form composed at a single location, and a much quieter and less disrupted text than *Little Books* or the *Journal*. Although it is the closest presentation of a "single" voice to be found in any of Weiner's publications over the past decade, the unsigned preface states that "*All* the words in this book were seen by Hannah Weiner first on her forehead" (emphasis mine), which is the first time this particular claim has been raised. Because other books have been fragmentary compilations selected from much larger writings (the selection of the *Journal* which Tom Ahern published as a chapbook contained all three pages of May 9, 1974, while the Angel Hair edition omits the first page), this volume has a sense of completion and closure to it not to be found elsewhere in her work. Even at 18 pages, its extension as a unit of writing goes beyond what is to be found in *Little Books/Indians* and most of the *Journal*.

IV ~~~~~

ZYXT

The last word (here, in English, in the OED): an obsolete Kentish form, the second person indicative present of the verb *see*. Language even ends in the eye. In a book, if we are enjoying ourselves, we often reduce our reading pace measurably in its final pages, luxuriating slowly in the joy of words and syntax (unlike that of ideas and referents, where the onset of the conclusion only accelerates the reading), anticipating an inevitable sadness which follows the end of the (always erotic) body of the text. The book closed sets loose an emotion tinged with jealousy and grief: its presence (which includes our own reflected in the text) is something we can never again possess. Rereading is not the same: words harden, aura crystallizing to define a wall no quantity of inspection can penetrate. In this afterword we sense ever so briefly the immense relief we felt in having been delivered awhile from the weight of directing our own psyches. This is the restorative value of any text (reading is a kind of sleep, a return to the senses). Now we can only wait until this wave of sorrow subsides before seeking the seduction of another book. There is no alternative. You zyxt.

FOOTNOTES

DISAPPEARANCE OF THE WORD, APPEARANCE OF THE WORLD

1. *Shaking the Pumpkin: Traditional Poetry of the Indian North Americans,* edited by Jerome Rothenberg (Doubleday Anchor, 1971), p. 341.

2. René Welleck and Austin Warren, *Theory of Literature* (Peregrine Books, 1963), p. 158.

3. *The Anchor Anthology of Sixteenth Century Verse,* edited by Richard Sylvester (Doubleday Anchor, 1974), p. 69.

4. Ludwig Wittgenstein, *Philosophical Investigations,* translated by G.E.M. Anscombe (MacMillan, 1953), p. 17.

5. Bertran H. Bronson, *Printing as an Index of Taste in Eighteenth Century England* (New York Public Library, 1958), p. 17.

THE POLITICAL ECONOMY OF POETRY

1. *Contemporaries and Snobs* (Cape, 1928), pp. 123-99.

2. (Verso Press, 1978), pp. 110-24.

3. *Marxism and the Philosophy of Language,* Translated by Ladislav Matejka and I.R. Titunik (Seminar Press, 1973) pp. 94-5.

4. (Penguin Books, 1949), pp. 142-3.

5. "Caricature," unpublished manuscript, p. 21

6. J. Kendrick Noble, Jr., "Books," in *Who Owns the Media,* edited by Benjamin Compaine (Harmony, 1979), p. 257.

7. "Conventions and Membership," in *PMLA,* Vol. 99, No. 3, May, 1984, p. 456.

8. *Classes in Contemporary Capitalism,* translated by David Fernbach (Verso Press, 1978), p. 323.

9. *Ibid.,* p. 311.

10. *Class, Crisis and the State* (Verso Press, 1979), pp. 108-9

11. Edited by Daniel Halpern (Avon, 1975).

1. Jean-Paul Sartre, *Life/Situations,* translated by Paul Auster and Lydia Davis (Pantheon, 1977), p. 40.

2. Walter Benjamin, "The Work of Art in the Age of Mechanical Reproduction," in *Illuminations,* edited by Hannah Arendt, translated by Harry Zohn (Shocken, 1969), p. 217. Hereafter cited as *Work.*

3. *Work,* p. 217, emphasis mine.

4. William Wordsworth, "Preface to *Lyrical Ballads*" in *Selected Poems and Prefaces,* edited by Jack Stillinger (Houghton Mifflin, 1965), p. 453.

5. *Work,* p. 217.

6. *Ibid.*

7. *Work,* pp. 217–8.

8. John Berger, *The Look of Things,* (Viking, 1974), p. 87.

9. *Marxism and Form* (Princeton, 1971), p. 60.

10. *Ibid.,* p. 74.

11. Hannah Arendt, "Introduction" to *Illuminations,* p. 11.

12. Karl Marx, *The 18th Brumaire of Louis Bonaparte* (International Publishers, 1963), p. 46.

13. *Ibid.,* 47.

14. Quoted in *Marxism and Literature* by Raymond Williams (Oxford University Press, 1977), p. 75.

15. Karl Marx, *Capital,* edited by Frederick Engels, translated by Samuel Moore and Edward Aveling, revised and amplified by Ernest Untermann (Modern Library, 1906), p. 467.

16. These ideas converge in Lacan's equation for the structure of the sign S/s, in which the bar between the signifier (S) and signified (s) represents precisely this gap.

17. *Work,* p. 218.

18. *Work,* p. 219.

19. *Ibid.* This is a questionable stance, in that the printing press proved a conceptual model for machinery as such.

20. *Ibid.*

21. *Ibid.*

22. Walter Benjamin, "A Short History of Photography," translated by Phil Patton, *Artform,* February, 1977, p. 47. Hereafter cited as *History.*

23. *Ibid.*, p. 48.

24. *Work*, pp. 219–20.

25. *Ibid.*, pp. 220–1.

26. Jacques Derrida *Of Grammatology*, translated by Gayatri Spivak (John Hopkins University Press, 1976), p. 310.

27. *Work*, pp. 220–1.

28. *Ibid.*, pp. 222–3, emphasis mine.

29. *History*, p. 49, emphasis mine.

30. Walter Benjamin, "On Some Motifs in Baudelaire," in *Illuminations*, p. 186.

31. *Ibid.*, p. 186.

32. *Ibid.*, p. 188.

33. *Ibid.*, p. 200.

34. *Work*, p. 222.

35. *Ibid.*, p. 223.

36. *Ibid.*

37. *Ibid.*

38. Ludwig Wittgenstein, *Tractatus Logico-Philosophicus*, translated by D.F. Pears and B.F. McGuinness, introduction by Bertrand Russell (Routledge and Kegan Paul, 1961), p. 5.

39. Lawrence Sklar, *Space, Time and Spacetime* (University of California Press, 1974), p. 14. This particular wording is Sklar's.

40. *Capital*, pp. 85–7.

41. Roland Barthes, *Image/Music/Text*, translated by Stephen Heath (Hill & Wang, 1977), p. 17 , Hereafter cited as *IMT*.

42. *Work*, p. 224.

43. *Ibid.*

44. *Ibid.*, p. 225.

45. *History*, p. 49.

46. *Work*, p. 226.

47. Susan Bee (Laufer), "Man Ray, Moholy-Nagy and Photograms," unpublished master's thesis, Hunter College, CUNY, 1977, p. 2. Hereafter cited as *Holograms*.

48. *IMT*, pp. 16–7.

49. *Holograms*, p. 7.

50. *Ibid.*, p. 19.

51. *Ibid.*, p. 20.

52. Herbert Marcuse, *Eros and Civilization* (Random House, 1955), p. 29.

53. *Work*, p. 225.

OF THEORY, TO PRACTICE

1. Cited in Ferruccio Rossi-Landi, *Linguistics and Economics* (Mouton, 1975), p. 5.

2. "To Define," *A Quick Graph: Collected Notes & Essays* (Four Seasons Foundation, 1970), p. 23.

3. "Poems are a complex," *A Quick Graph*, p. 54.

4. "T.E. Hulme, the New Barbarians, & Gertrude Stein," in *Contemporaries and Snobs*, (Cape, 1928), pp. 123-99.

THE NEW SENTENCE

1. P. 90.

2. Adapted from p. 91.

3. Ed Friedman, *The Telephone book* (Power Mad Press/Telephone Books, 1979), p. 145.

4. Ferdinand de Saussure, *Course in General Linguistics*, edited by Charles Bally and Albert Sechehaye in collaboration with Albert Riedlinger, translated by Wade Baskin (McGraw-Hill, 1966), p. 106. The terms in brackets are mine.

5. *Ibid.*, p. 124.

6. *Ibid.*, p. 128.

7. Noam Chomsky, *Aspects of the Theory of Syntax* (MIT Press, 1965), pp. 17-8.

8. Simeon Potter, *Modern Linguistics* (Norton, 1964), pp. 104-5.

9. Translated by Ladislav Matejka and I.R. Titunik (Seminar Press, 1973), pp. 109-10.

10. Translated by G.E.M. Anscombe (McMillian Co., 1953) pp. 138e-9e.

11. (Dover, 1952), p. 8.

12. J.L. Austin, *Sense and Sensibilia*, reconstructed from the manuscript notes by G.J. Warnock (Oxford University Press, 1964), p. 110n.

13. (MIT Press, 1960), pp. 191-3.

14. (Peregrine Books, 1963), p. 153, emphasis mine.

15. *Ibid.*

16. Vol. XIX, No. 4, p. 99.

17. "Language and Literature," in *The Structuralist Controversy*, edited by Richard Macksey and Eugenio Donata (John Hopkins University Press, 1972), 130.

18. "To Write: Intransitive Verb?" *ibid.*, p. 136.

19. Translated by Annette Lavers and Colin Smith (HIll & Wang, 1968), pp. 44-7.

20. "Postmodernism, or The Cultural Logic of Late Capitalism," in *New Left Review*, No. 146, July/August, 1984, p. 71.

21. Volosinov, *Op. Cit.*, p. 111.

22. "Plasma," in *Plasma/Paralleles/"X"* (Tuumba, 1979), no pagination.

23. *Ibid.*

24. *Ibid.*

25. (Doubleday Anchor, 1953), pp. 75-6.

26. *Edson's Mentality* (Oink! Press, 1977), p. 21.

27. *The Poems* (Penguin Books, 1977), p. 217.

28. (Edward McCann), p. 538.

29. Included in *Imaginations*, edited by Webster Schott (New Directions, 1970), p. 70.

30. *Writing and Lectures: 1909-1945*, edited by Patricia Meyerowitz (Penguin Books, 1971), p. 189.

31. (Something Else Press, 1973), pp. 26-32.

32. *Ibid.*, p. 132 and 149.

33. *Ibid.*, p. 166-7.

34. *Writings and Lectures, op. cit.*, pp. 130 and 133-4.

35. *Ibid.*, p. 137.

36. In *United Artists Five*, December, 1978, no pagination.

37. (The Figures, 1984), p. 1.

38. From the series "Celestial Mechanics" in *Cafe Isotope* (The Figures, 1980), p. 1.

39. *Under the Bridge* (This Press, 1980), pp. 57-8.

40. "Postmodernism, or the Cultural Logic of Late Capitalism," *op. cit.*, p. 73.

41. "Plasma," *op. cit.*

1. Translated by Louise Varese (New Directions, 1970), pp. ix–x.

2. (Laurel, 1976).

3. (Cambridge University Press, 1983).

4. "The Prose of Fact," in *Talks: Hills* 6/7, 1980, p. 168.

5. "After Sentence, Sentence," in *The American Book Review*, Vol. 4, No. 6, September–October, 1982, p. 3.

6. Cited by Roland Barthes in *Writing Degree Zero*, translated by Annette Lavers and Colin Smith (Hill & Wang), p. 41.

7. *Selected Poems and Prefaces*, edited by Jack Stillinger (Houghton Mifflin, 1965), p. 451n.

8. (Peregrine Books, 1963) p. 158, emphasis mine..

9. *The Poetics of Prose*, translated by Richard Howard (Cornell University Press, 1977), p. 35.

10. "paradise/our/speech," in *A Quick Graph*, edited by Donald Allen (Four Seasons Foundation, 1970), p. 124.

11. *Course in General Linguistics*, edited by Charles Bally and Albert Sechehaye in collaboration with Albert Riedlinger, translated by Wade Baskin (McGraw Hill, 1966), pp. 23–30, emphasis mine.

12. Linda R. Waugh, "The Poetic Function in the Theory of Roman Jakobson," in *Poetics Today*, Vol 2. No. 1a, p. 59.

13. *Ibid.*, p. 57.

14. *Ibid.*, p. 58.

15. "Poetry and Abstact Thought," translated by Denise Folliot, in *Paul Valery: An Anthology*, selected by James R. Lawler (Bollingen, 1977), pp. 154–6.

16. Cited in Denns Keene, *The Modern Japanese Prose Poem* (Princeton, 1980), p. 40.

17. *Of Grammatology*, translated by Gayatri Spivak (Johns Hopkins University Press, 1976), p. 29.

18. *Six Lectures on Sound and Meaning*, translated by John Mepham (MIT Press, 1978), pp. 46–7.

19. *Ibid.*, pp. 63–5, emphasis mine.

20. *Ibid.*, p. 65.

21. "An Analysis of Graphemes as a System," unpublished manuscript, p. 4.

22. *Op. cit.*, p. 45.

23. "On Speech," Winter, 1971, no pagination.

MIGRATORY MEANING

1. "Cabin Fever," p. 297.

2. *Ibid.*

3. Victor Erlich, *Russian Formalism: History—Doctrine*, Third Edition (Yale University Press, 1981), pp. 190–1.

4. "The Work of Art in the Age of Mechanical Reproduction," in *Illuminations*, edited by Hannah Arendt, translated by Harry Zohn (Shocken, 1969), p. 276.

5. *Oakland*, (Tuumba Press, 1980), no pagination.

6. John Searle, *Speech Acts*, (Cambridge University Press, 1969), p. 119.

7. *The Pound Era* (University of California Press, 1971), p. 184.

8. Charles J. Fillmore, "Ideal Readers and Real Readers," mimeograph, 1981, p.16.

9. *Ibid.*, p. 13.

10. In Theory of Prose but cited in this translation in Pavel Medvedev and Mikhail Bakhtin, *The Formal Method in Literary Scholarship: A Critical Introduction* (Johns Hopkins University Press, 1978), p. 89.

12. *Extremities* (The Figures, 1978), p. 13.

13. *Philosophical Grammar* (University of California Press, 1978), p. 69.

14. *Down and Back* (The Figures, 1978), pp. 16–7.

15. "Language-Centered," in $L=A=N=G=U=A=G=E$, Vol. 4, (published in cooperation with *Open Letter*), 1981, pp. 23–6.

16. Fillmore, *op. cit.*, p. 7.

17. This follows a definition given by Paul Kay.

18. "The Indeterminate Interval: From History to Blur," in $L=A=N=G=U=A=G=E$, Vol. 4, pp. 31–9.

19. Althusser, "Ideology and Ideological State Apparatuses," in *Lenin and Philosophy*, (Monthly Review Press, 1971), and Therborn, *The Ideology of Power and the Power of Ideology* (Verso Press, 1980).

20. *Theory of Prose* (Cornell University Press, forthcoming).

21. *The Tennis Court Oath* (Wesleyan University Press, 1962), p. 33.

22. *The Logical Structure of Linguistic Theory* (Plenum Press, 1975), pp. 94–5.

23. *Ibid.*, p. 95.

24. *7 Work* (The Figures, 1978), pp. 87, 89.

25. *Controlling Interests* (Roof, 1980), pp. 37–8, and *Senses of Responsibility* (Tuumba Press, 1979), no pagination, respectively.

26. *Op. cit.*, p. 95.

27. (The Figures Press, 1978).

28. *Down and Back, op. cit.*, p. 11.

29. (Burning Deck, 1980).

30. In *Hills* 8, 1981, p. 87.

31. *Ibid.*, p. 98.

Z-SITED PATH

1. "Poem," *The Collected Earlier Poems of William Carlos Williams* (New Directions, 1951), p. 340.

2. Vol. 44, No. 4, July, 1934, pp. 220–1.

3. George Oppen, *Collected Poems* (New Directions, 1975), p. 45. The poem was originally collected in *The Materials*, published in 1962.

4. *Ibid.*, p. 229. The poem was written around 1972.

5. *Ibid.*, p. 178.

6. (University of California Press, 1982).

7. *Ibid.*, p. 75.

8. *Ibid.*, p. 223.

9 *Ibid.*, p. 227.

10. *Ibid.*, p. 141.

11. *Ibid.*, p. 102.

12. *Ibid.*, p. 103. Ahearn takes this from Zukofsky's "About the Gas Age" *Prepositions* (University of California Press, 1981), p. 170, where, in context, the statement carries markedly different connotations.

13. Ahearn, *ibid.*, p. 104.

14. *First Half of "A"-9* (Privately Printed, 1940), p. 41.

1. *The Collected Books of Jack Spicer*, edited by Robin Blaser (Black Sparrow, 1975), p. 217.

2. *Ibid.*, p. 57-8.

3. *The Cantos (1-95)* (New Directions, 1956), pp. 115-6.

4. Only in the following poem, "Sporting Life," will it become apparent that "signals" is setting up one of the major figures in *Language*, the poet as radio.

5. As is the case with several contemporary French poets.

6. "Vancouver Lecture #1" in *Caterpillar* 12, July, 1970, pp. 204-5.

7. *Reflections on Language* (Pantheon, 1975), p. 51.

8. *Collected Books, op. cit.*, p. 152.

9. *Ibid.*, p. 164.

10. *Ibid.*, p. 175.

11. *Arthur Rimbuad: Collected Works*, translated by Paul Schmidt (Harper & Row, 1975), p. 100. Rimbaud's conception of the medium is more transparent than Spicer's. It is worth noting that this passage introduces the homoerotic poem "The Stolen Heart" ("Soldiers' cocks are a black burlesque;/They rape my heart with what they say"), of which Rimbaud comments to Izambard, in a phrase that anticipates the first poem of "Thing Language," "That does not mean nothing."

12. "Vancouver Lecture #1," *op. cit.*, p. 204-5.

13. *Ibid.*, p. 179.

CONTROLLING INTERESTS

1. *Poetics Journal*, No. 3, May, 1983, p. 6.

2. *The Collected Poems of Robert Creeley: 1945-1975* (University of California Press, 1982), p. 140.

3. The quotations in this section are all from this poem, in *Controlling Interests* (Roof, 1980), pp. 48-50.

4. The term "natural narrative" is used, following William Labov, in Mary Louise Pratt's *Toward a Speech Act Theory of Literary Discourse*.

5. That this allusion is intentional is best demonstrated by contrasting it with an even larger paraphrase from the work of Marcuse in the next passage, "To sustain such blows and/undermine the lash is memory's

cure." While Bernstein could have used this to equally point to the tradition of philosophy, he doesn't. Neither philosphy nor memory are major issues here, and Bernstein is sensitive to the degree to which he is willing to raise them. Just the opposite is the case with love, portrayal and objectification—and it is here that the poem *insists*.

6. *Op. cit.*, pp. 15-6.

INDEX

page numbers for quotations are in italics

Weiner, Hannah, 88, 185–88

Welch, Lew, 23, 129, 132

Wellek, René, 9, 25, *Theory of Literature*, 22–23, 72–74, 98

Wertmeuller, Lina, 8

Whalen, Philip, 132

Wheatley, Phyllis, 171

Whitman, Walt, 13, *Leaves of Grass*, 34

Whole (non-existence of the), 122–23

Wieners, John, 132

Wilbur, Richard, 132

Wilde, Oscar, 82

Williams, Raymond, 37

Williams, William Carlos, 58, 96, 108, 128–36, *137*, 140–41, 162, *Collected Earlier Poems*, 24, *Kora in Hell: Improvisations*, 63, *83–84*, 95, *Paterson*, 128,

Spring & All, 23–24, 58, 157, *The Wedge*, 23

Wittgenstein, Ludwig, *114*, *Philosophical Investigations*, 11, 70, *Tractatus Logico-Philosophicus*, 47, 70, *161*

Woolf, Douglas, 14

Wordsworth, William, 101, *Lyrical Ballads*, *34*, 97, *107–8*

Wright, Erik Olin, *28*

Wright, James, 87, 95–96

Writing (vs. language), 98–108

Yeats, William Butler, 60

Zukofsky, Celia, *L.Z. Masque*, 137

Zukofsky, Louis, 74, 98, 127–28, 132–33, 136–37, 142–46, 168, 200

Zukofsky, Paul, 142

209

Made in the USA
Monee, IL
06 October 2024